BEGINNING AND GROWTH

OF

THE CHRISTIAN LIFE;

OR,

THE SUNDAY-SCHOOL TEACHER.

"Herein is my Father glorified, that ye bear much fruit; so shall ye be my disciples."

FOURTH EDITION.

BOSTON:
AMERICAN UNITARIAN ASSOCIATION.
1867.

NOTICE.

THE Directors of the Sunday-School Society think proper to accompany the works which appear under their sanction with a brief statement of the views by which they are guided.

It is their desire to aid in circulating books that may promote the love of God and man, books that may reliably assist the teacher in his important work, or give to the pupil lessons in harmony with the law of Christ. No work will be published by them which does not, in their opinion, fulfil these conditions. They will neither cause to be printed, nor otherwise recommend, books inconsistent with a Christianity at once liberal and evangelical. But they do not consider themselves responsible for minor peculiarities of sentiment or expression. Writers equally intelligent and pious may differ in these. It is better that each should utter his own thought, even if sometimes inaccurate, than that all individuality should be destroyed by a too unsparing criticism.

CONTENTS.

THE CHRISTIAN LIFE.

CHAPTER I.

INTRODUCTORY REMARKS.

"Fold of the tender Shepherd! rise, and spread!
Arch o'er our frailty roofs of everlasting strength!
Be all the body gathered to its living Head!
Wanderers we faint; O, let us find our Lord at length!

DURING the last few years, observing persons can hardly have watched with any degree of attention the progress of events, without feeling that great and important changes have been and still are taking place in the religious, no less than in the social and political world.

More silently, unnoticed by the common observer it may be, but none the less surely, has the old order of things been passing away; and to the earnest seeker there are significant tokens prophetical of a new era in sects and parties of the Church.

Ideals of a better and higher state, longings for a more Christ-like life and a more spiritual union, a consciousness that creeds and dogmas have too often usurped the place of an inward faith and a practical piety, that disciples have breathed far too little of their Master's spirit of love, forbearance, and humility, that the Church of Christ even has been too often untrue to her noble mission and high calling, — such thoughts fill at times every reflecting and thoughtful mind, and prompt the earnest question, "By what means is a higher spiritual life to be attained? How is the true coming of Christ's kingdom to be promoted?"

Look into our Sabbath schools, regarded now, and for many years past, as established Christian institutions. Acknowledging freely and fully all the good that has been accomplished, all the pure and holy influences that have flowed from them, as fruitful sources of religious instruction and spiritual life, — recalling, too, with grateful remembrance, the many pure, devoted, and consecrated spirits that have faithfully labored in this portion of their Master's vineyard, — it is not to be denied that in many quarters there is a prevalent dissatisfaction, a feeling that such schools are not accomplishing their highest ends.

Progress, indeed, there has been; but has the advance been commensurate with our means, opportunities, and privileges? Do our schools, as now conducted, meet the deepest wants of the youthful spirit? Does the young heart there find that bread of Life, which will alone satisfy its cravings amid the sterner trials of maturer years? Are teachers laboring upon the right principles, or has the true end been too often lost sight of in mere external or mechanical forms? Are we to rest contentedly where we are, feel that no onward steps are to be taken, and quietly and inanely yield ourselves to the force of surrounding circumstances, or are we not rather to make some strenuous, earnest effort to seek a higher plane of action, to spiritualize our endeavors, and to render our schools more completely Christian institutions?

In the words of another, "There is among men of earnest and reverent moods a pause and an expectation, as if they heard a divine voice just becoming articulate and audible, — coming, not out of the old creeds, but out of the Divine Word, and out of the most interior consciousness of men, and prophesying of the things that are yet to be."

In all our churches there are young hearts questioning the truth of the dogmas inculcated from childhood, and earnestly asking the meaning of the great doctrines of man's sinfulness and redemption, of pardon, salvation, and retribution. In all our churches there are souls that earnestly long to know their relations to Christ as a personal Saviour, — that ask not for forms or systems, or an intellectual belief, but for *Christ*; for his cross, as a seal of their own acceptance; for his death, as a pledge of their pardon.

Are these wants truly met among us? Are they always even fully acknowledged? Read the words and ponder the deep meaning of those expressions applied to Christ, both by himself and his Apostles, marking him as divine in his nature, power, and authority, and then say whether it be sufficient to the young and aspiring soul, hungering and thirsting after righteousness, longing for an assurance of faith and hope, to be brought to him, as is too often the case, as a holy teacher and guide alone? Is there not a deeper craving of the soul, which cannot and will not thus be satisfied?

Go into any of our larger towns or cities; explore carefully the narrow streets, the crowded houses, the lanes and cellars; see the iniquity and sin, the ignorance, degradation, and heathenism that exist under the very shadow of our churches and schools, and will not the question force itself upon the mind, Are these indeed *Christian* communities?

Do we not need some new power at work among us, — some voice to vitalize the dry bones of a barren and self-sufficient piety, of frigid naturalism, of unbelief and misbelief, — some prophet's touch to rouse the dead body of the Church to a new and Christ-like life?

Do we not need some new outpouring of the Holy Spirit, and a renewed and quickened faith in the power and efficacy of prayer? Have we a vital, practical belief in the promised influences of the Spirit, in the assurance that if we ask anything according to the Father's will, He will hear and answer the petition?

Abstractions, forms and creeds, the mere inculcation of facts, or intellectual teaching alone, will not satisfy; and individual souls are earnestly looking for a better administration, for some nobler and higher development of faith and love.

What part, then, has the Sunday school to perform in meeting, in any good degree, these wants and needs? What should be the true aim and object of its instructions? How are its highest ends to be sustained and carried out? How is it to be rendered an efficient co-worker with the Church, in the regeneration of individual souls, in leading young hearts to Christ, as the only sufficient, the divinely appointed Mediator and Redeemer?

Questions such as these, prompted by no momentary impulse of excitement or discouragement, but proceeding from various and widely separated quarters, demand the due consideration and serious reflection of every individual interested in the welfare of the Church, or engaged in the sacred calling of the Christian teacher.

The future, and the future alone, can and will bear true and enduring witness, whether they are now faithfully met and answered.

CHAPTER II.

THE WANTS OF OUR SUNDAY SCHOOLS.

"As the branch cannot bear fruit of itself, except it abide in the vine, no more can ye, except ye abide in me."

"And still in accents sweet and strong,
Sounds, as of old, the word:
More laborers for the harvest, *now!*
More reapers for the Lord!"

THE present state of our Sunday schools in different denominations may be regarded under two distinct aspects. The general, careless observer, content with mere outward appearance, and satisfied with statistical results, would tell us of the increased number of such institutions, of the multiplication of the pupils, the books studied, the popularity of this or that teacher, the successful annual celebration, and the apparent general interest manifested in the concerns of the school. He would congratulate the pupils upon their advantages, tell them how much greater their privileges than those enjoyed by preceding generations, and, satisfied with having given his meed of praise, rest contentedly in the belief that little more is needed, and that it would be both unwise and unreasonable to expect greater or more definite results.

To the observant eye and thoughtful mind, even a cursory view would lead to a far different conclusion. Accustomed to a higher stand-point, looking beneath the mere exterior and surface of things, he would find abundant food for careful investigation and serious thought. He would see wants to be met, defects to be remedied, plans to be reorganized, a living spirit to be infused, and a nobler and higher end to be achieved.

Regardless of statistical information or of any reputed worth, he would compare the true spirit of these institutions with the spirit of Christ, and acknowledge their actual value and importance just so far as they breathed the spirit and manifested the power of the religion of Jesus of Nazareth.

How, then, we would freely ask, can our schools be rendered more conducive to their true ends? What are some of their most prominent wants and defects? What changes are truly and pressingly needed among us?

First, we would speak of the time usually set apart for such religious instruction.

The greater part of six days of the week is devoted by the pupils of our Sabbath schools to studies of a secular nature, guided by those who have long been preparing for their work, and whose whole time and best energies are given to its faithful prosecution. Why should all the direct religious instruction received by them, apart from religious home influences, upon all the vast themes of eternity and immortality, be confined to one single hour of the Sabbath? Even then the teacher sometimes affirms that "the school has been too long, and that the pupils are weary"!

To have any systematic, definite course of instruction pursued, and more worthy ends accomplished, the school should not be crowded into a single hour of the Sabbath. More time should be sacredly set apart for it, and during that portion of the day when both mind and body are fresh and vigorous. To have all the general exercises of the school, — reading, singing, often some address from the pastor or superintendent, the direct instruction in the classes, the exchange of library books, &c., — comprised in a single hour, seems utterly without reason. To pass from the morning service at church to the duties of the school, then to attend a second service, and perhaps a Bible class, once a month the communion service intervening, with hardly a half hour's intermission, is rendering that a mere task-work, and often a mere mechanical form, which demands the freshest energies and the exercise of the best powers of the soul. Indeed, from the manner of some, it would seem as if they imagined that the greater the amount of such labor accomplished on the Sabbath the greater the merit, forgetting that a spiritual worship demands a spiritual preparation, and that no class of children, however young or ignorant, can be truly instructed and interested where there is a conscious mental weariness or indifference on the part of the teacher.

Whatever the amount of time any school may see fit to set apart for religious instruction, — and this, of course, must somewhat vary with different places and different customs of society, — we would strongly advocate the *morning* hours during the year being sacredly devoted to this work.

Let *at least an hour and a half* be thus secured, and a new impulse, we doubt not, would be given to the efficiency of many of our schools. Let the children assemble when a hurried dinner is just over, or at the close of the afternoon service, and it requires little observation to mark the difference between the apparent interest then taken in the exercises, and that manifested during the fresh morning hour, when there is no weariness or listlessness. "What! is our morning school to be closed so soon?" exclaimed a bright-eyed little girl as her teacher informed her of the usual change of hours on the succeeding Sabbath. "I know I have a long walk to take, but if all of us can get to school at nine o'clock on week days, I do n't see why we cannot come at the same hour on Sundays; our morning schools are so much pleasanter!"

Might not such an end be attained in many instances, and punctuality secured, by a deeper interest and a little effort on the part of parents, and perchance by a little sacrifice of indulgence or ease on the part of teachers? One hour of the time thus set apart we would have exclusively devoted to direct instruction in the classes; the remaining portion to be occupied by prayer, the reading of the Scriptures, either by the superintendent alone or alternately with the pupils, accompanied by some simple exposition, singing, and occasionally an address from the pastor, superintendent, or some competent person.

Next, we would earnestly and solemnly utter our protest against the tendency, too common, of rendering our schools mere places of *amusement* to children. Religious instruction should, indeed, be rendered cheerful, interesting, and attractive; but to degrade religion from its native dignity, to divest it of its eternal importance and solemnity, in order to excite the momentary smile or laugh by some undignified illustration, or a mere familiar, off-hand manner of address, or to occupy the limited time by mere story-telling, or a vague, rambling talk, without point or force, is utterly unworthy the sacred hours of the Sabbath, and the object of the school. No one should ever attempt to address a school unless he has some definite idea in his own mind of what he wishes to say, and then his words should be simple, brief, serious, and to the point

Children cannot be too deeply or too early impressed with the *solemn reverence* due to all the themes of religion; and where this is in any measure violated, an infinite wrong is done to the cause of truth and holiness. Were those few solemn words of the Saviour's, "God is a Spirit, and they who worship him must worship him in spirit and in truth," ever to be remembered by those who conduct such institutions, and by all engaged as teachers,—were they to know from experience what is meant by

"The perfect power of *godliness*,
The omnipotence of love,"

we believe that all tendency to flippancy and lightness, ever to be deprecated by every serious mind, would soon disappear.

"The effort," says another, "sometimes seems to be, not so much to lift the infant spirit up to heaven, as to draw the dread majesty of heaven down to earth, and to place in the child's mind an entire and satisfying image of the unseen and eternal Jehovah. It is deemed not enough that he should worship,—he must thoroughly comprehend, the divine nature and attributes. It should be borne in mind, that the distinct and satisfying ideas of infancy are early outgrown; and if the idea of God no more than fills the narrow walls of the infant spirit, it will not grow with the growth of the mind, but will soon be outgrown and cast into contemptuous oblivion. If the idea of unsearchableness and immensity be sustained in the child's mind, and with every new stage of progress the feeling be impressed, 'Lo, these are parts of his ways, but how little a portion is heard of him,' then there is indefinite room for the conception of God to expand with the growth of the mind, and still for the devout emotions to have a field reaching beyond that of clear vision and distinct thought, far away into infinity."

Let religious truths be rendered attractive, but attractive through their own innate grandeur, dignity, and worth; impressive, through their infinite importance and solemn message to the individual soul. Such instructions, and such only, do we need; for only truths thus presented, ministering to the highest wants and deepest cravings of the soul, will render our schools places of vital religious growth, and a true spiritual nurture.

The devotional exercises, also, should be such as to promote this same feeling of reverence, to quicken faith, and to deepen and strengthen the love of prayer in the hearts of the pupils. Whether this result can best be attained by the use of responses, or otherwise, the true and ultimate end is one and the same.

In whatever outward form the prayer is offered, its language should be at once reverential and simple, adapted to the capacities of the pupils, and embodying such petitions as may bear upon their peculiar temptations, wants, and spiritual needs. In many schools, such is far from being the case. The language used is too often entirely above their comprehension, and the petitions such as are adapted to the wants of an adult congregation rather than to the impulsive hearts of children. They understand not the words, and, as a natural result, feel that it is a mere form, belonging to the teachers rather than to themselves, and in which they have no part to take. Often, wearied with the length of the exercise, they become restless and uneasy, and prayer, instead of being regarded as a holy and delightful privilege, becomes a tedious and barren form. In adapting the words of the prayer to the capacities of the child, it is not necessary in any way to lessen its devout reverence; — for what exercise of the school is more solemn or important than that of approaching in supplication Him before whom the very heavens are not clean? Let the petitions, thanksgiving, and praise, the supplication for strength and help, and the divine blessing through the Redeemer, be brief, concise, and heart-felt. Let them be clothed in simple, yet always in the most reverential language, and let one of the first lessons in every school be, to impress on the minds of the pupils the solemnity of this portion of the service, the part they are to take in it, and the inestimable privilege of being thus permitted, in their weakness and ignorance, to approach the Father of all. Brevity is of all-essential importance in this service. A prayer of three or four minutes is far more impressive than one of ten, to a child; — and may we not add, to the teacher also?

Where the peculiar "gift of prayer" is wanting in superintendent or teacher, so that he cannot rely upon the promptings of the moment to express his deepest thoughts, let some simple form be prepared, to which he may always turn for assistance.

What is wanting more than all is the true spirit of prayer, — a personal sense of dependence on the Saviour, and a devout, reverential trust and faith in the Father. Where such a spirit exists, the general prayer, whether it be in the words of an oft-repeated form, or the spontaneous expression of the moment, simple, confiding, and child-like, cannot but be uttered in such a manner as to attract and fix the attention of the school.

As this exercise is now conducted in many of our schools, it needs no keen observation to see what a mere ceremony it is to the greater part of the pupils. The baneful influence to the individual of such habits of inattention, of spiritual listlessness, of wandering thoughts, and cold irreverence, cannot be overestimated.

A decided change is needed. If prayer be a divine ordinance, if it be the privilege and duty of every soul to approach in supplication the Father of spirits, to bring before the Eternal its wants and desires, fears and aspirations, let us have, at least in schools dedicated to His service and bearing the Saviour's name, some mode of conducting this sacred service more hallowed and more impressive. No matter how brief, no matter how simple, if it be reverential, devout, earnest, and sincere. The most impressive prayers in which we have ever joined in any school were those clothed in language so simple that every child could understand their meaning, and yet so devout, so earnest, so solemn and impressive, that a feeling of awe and hushed reverence stole irresistibly over the spirit, as it felt in whose presence it stood.

An abundance of words, a repetition of phrases, or numerous subjects of entreaty, are not needed to give force and impressiveness to this act. A few brief petitions fervently and earnestly uttered will dwell in the heart when a longer form would all be forgotten. Spiritual life there must be, or prayer will ever become a mere form; spiritual earnestness and sincerity there must be, or the petitions offered will all be devoid of meaning; spiritual communion with the Saviour there must be, for he alone leads us to the Father, as the Way, Truth, and Life.

There is still another want in our schools, more obvious perhaps to the general eye, and one which in some way must be speedily met and remedied, — a want not confined to any one sect or denomination, but common in a greater or less degree to all; namely, a sufficient number of *competent* teachers.

Judging in the abstract, with no definite knowledge or personal acquaintance with the details of the system, we should at once suppose that wherever a Christian congregation was gathered, there would be found an abundant supply of all the materials requisite to conduct such a school, and to render it what it ever should be, an institution for the Christian nurture of children and youth. We should imagine that no command of the Great Shepherd would be more readily fulfilled, than that of faithfully feeding the sheep and lambs of his flock; of seeking to bring the ignorant, the degraded, the homeless, and the prodigal into his sheltering fold. But a knowledge of the actual and existing state of things leads to a far different result. Many there are earnestly, faithfully, and sincerely engaged in this work, but the supply of willing, able, and competent teachers is far less than the demand. What proportion, indeed, do the teachers, in most of our schools, bear to the entire adult congregation, or to those not detained by more pressing home duties from taking a part in the work; and of that proportion, why is it that so few are from the busy scenes of life, — those whose position and calling would at once make their influence felt, — the men of business and education, of science and letters? Is the employment beneath their notice? Is it simply a matter of indifference, or do they really doubt its utility and efficiency?

A plea of unfitness for the work, or of want of time, is seldom a sincere excuse; for, were its importance actually felt, those alive on other subjects to their individual responsibility would not be backward in seeking, at least, to prepare themselves for this noble vocation; and want of time is seldom offered as an excuse in any worldly calling, where pleasure, or gain, or preferment is the expected reward.

Go into almost any school, and you will find some class without any permanent teacher; the more advanced pupils often asking in vain for those who can lead them on in their studies, and guide their inquiries, and help their examination of the truth.

Often does the entire superintendence of the school devolve on the pastor, whose duties in the pulpit exhaust his energies, and tax his powers, and who ought never to feel *obliged* to undertake these additional services on the Sabbath, however much his heart may be in th work.

"What am I to do?" said the faithful and devoted minister of one of our largest congregations, not long since. "Our valued superintendent removed from the city some months ago, and there is not a single individual in my parish upon whom I can call to fill the vacancy. True, there are some who would gladly seek this somewhat public post, but who are utterly unfitted for its duties; and those who seem capable of taking such a position are unwilling. What, then, can I do? Either the school must be closed, or I must be present to conduct its general exercises, besides having the instruction of a Bible class of young men. I shall continue these labors," he added, "so long as health and strength are granted, but if these fail, the school must seek some other support."

Is there not something radically wrong wherever this state of things exists? Is the pastor of the church the only one to offer the social prayer, and break the bread of life to his youthful flock? Ought he to be the only one capable of instructing the inquiring minds of those advancing to maturer years, and of leading them on to the higher phases of religious truth? Is there not a half-acknowledged feeling among many, and especially among men of business, that this work belongs only to the stated minister of the Gospel, or to a chosen and retired few, — that *they* have no responsibility with regard to it, — or that if they give pecuniary aid to the support of Christian institutions, they are wholly excused from giving what is of greater importance, their *personal* influence, example, and effort?

Will the fidelity of one, or of a few, excuse the indifference or negligence of the many? Had each individual statedly worshipping in our churches, and thus acknowledging, in outward form at least, his belief in Christ, sought faithfully to fulfil his own part in spreading the knowledge of a Saviour, would there be the heathenism that now exists beneath the very shadows of our churches and our homes? Do such reply, that little good comes of this instruction, and that they can accomplish nothing in this cause?

Let them look to the noble examples of those Christian men, whose patient perseverance, earnest effort, and devoted fidelity, have accomplished so much in rendering our schools in some degree what they should be, — men, not only faithful in the private walks of life, but taking a foremost part in all that concerns the public good, active in business, interested in the higher pur suits of literature, and yet always finding time to prepare themselves for the humblest duties of instruction, and entering into all the details of school duties with as much interest and zeal as if these constituted their sole employment.

Thankfully do we acknowledge the influence of all such now laboring in the field; and with gratitude would we remember those passed within the veil, but whose spiritual influence still dwells among us, and whose prayers and intercessions are still poured forth in behalf of a work so dear to them while here. Their memories will long be cherished in grateful and loving hearts; and whose but the All-seeing Eye can measure the extent of their Christian influence and trusting faith?

No: the Gospel offers no license to any class of men, or any individuals, to throw off their personal responsibilities on others. Each one must give account of himself unto God. Every disciple of Christ is called on to labor in some way in his vineyard, to aid in gathering in the harvest, waiting only for the faithful reapers,—for, "inasmuch as ye did it *not* to the least of these, my brethren, ye did it not to me."

We repeat, our schools demand more and better qualified teachers, if they are to be permanently sustained,—if they are truly to be co-workers with the Church in the regeneration of individual souls. Systematic, regular, and thorough instruction is needed; and to facilitate this end, we also pressingly need a higher order of manuals, and better works of illustration than are now generally used among us. We are aware that this want has been partially met by works published within the last two years, but still it is far from being fully supplied. And what field of labor more useful and more inviting than this, — demanding a practical experience in the office of teaching, united with the requisite intellectual and spiritual qualifications?

Again and again are the questions asked, How is the interest of the older pupils to be sustained? How are young men, especially, to be retained under our influence, and at the very age when they most need the restraining power of Christian institutions and Christian example? What means should be taken to bring the poorer and more ignorant classes of children under the influence of our best schools, and how may regularity of attendance and a true interest be secured among such?

Many and various are the answers that might be given to these questions. If a sufficient number of faithful and competent teachers were provided for every such institution, other difficulties would soon be overcome. In what the necessary qualifications consist we shall hereafter consider; in this chapter we have designed only to refer to the more prominent wants and defects of our schools.

In speaking of these wants, we would not be unmindful of the good hitherto accomplished by means of this agency, of the quickening and holy influences that ever react on the teacher's own soul, where the duty of instruction is undertaken with any vital feeling of its solemn and deep importance. We would remember those who have been rescued from lives of sin and ignominy, the many hearts that have been led to a deeper faith, a purer love, and a more spiritual walk and life through the simple, earnest words spoken from week to week by some faithful teacher, often unconscious how deeply his own spirit was impressing the youthful mind, apparently so thoughtless and unconcerned.

Fully and freely acknowledging the good, the question still recurs, Are our Sabbath schools all that they ought to be? Are they fulfilling their highest and only true end? Are they, in truth, *living* branches of the one true Vine?

CHAPTER III.

THE TRUE OBJECT OF SUNDAY-SCHOOL INSTRUCTION.

"I am the Way, the Truth, and the Life: no man cometh unto the Father but by me."

WHEN a teacher enters upon his duties, and voluntarily assumes the responsibilities of a spiritual guide and instructor of others, he has, or at least he ought to have, some definite idea of the objects to be attained, and of the means by which such ends may be accomplished.

The first, most important, and all-essential questions for him to ask himself, whether he has these duties in contemplation only, or has long been engaged in the work, are these: What *aim* am I to keep steadily in view? What should be the true object of my instruction and influence? Is it to implant religious knowledge only in the minds of those committed to my care, or to achieve still more the higher end of awakening in their souls a spiritual life, a personal love to the Saviour, and a profound individual trust and faith in the universal Father? Is it sufficient that I make a faithful intellectual preparation for my work, — make myself acquainted with its various details, and become familiar with its facts of geography, history, and chronology, — or is there not imperative a higher spiritual preparation, by which alone I can speak to the hearts of those under my care?

To impart religious knowledge alone to the mind of the child we deem of unspeakable importance; to make him clearly and definitely acquainted with the great facts and truths of religion, and with the foundation on which those truths rest, is doing a work which, accompanied by the divine blessing, may be sanctified to his eternal salvation. If such teaching be regular, systematic, and thorough, its importance cannot be over-estimated, for it is the best safeguard against superstition, and the foundation of all free, personal inquiry and conviction.

The simple hymns of childhood, and the verses of Scripture faithfully committed to memory, even when imperfectly understood, will often recur to the mind in after years, and repeat their lessons of warning, encouragement, and hope, in tones that will not and cannot be resisted. Amid scenes of pleasure and gayety, or of trial and grief, amid the festive throng, or in the hushed and darkened chamber of illness, in hours of stern temptation and bitter conflict, when manly strength is weakened, and the pride of human power laid low, or in the calm and quiet hour of repose, when the spirit of God moves over the soul, and says to every unholy passion, "Peace, be still"; then will these words of truth often return with irresistible power, and become the medium by which the Spirit speaks to the soul, ever repeating these blessed words of encouragement and entreaty, "Whosoever will, let him freely come."

We repeat, the importance of imparting religious knowledge, if the teacher be thoroughly and faithfully fitted for his work, cannot be over-estimated. Take a child from a home of misery and sin, of ignorance and degradation, bring him under the influence of a well-regulated and orderly school, and if he only learns to repeat the Lord's Prayer, and the simple words, "Thou God seest me," it will not have been wholly in vain. Some spiritual power will be quickened, some dormant feeling aroused, some higher purpose enkindled. The very words, "Our Father, who art in heaven," will at some time awaken an inquiring thought, and a desire to learn of that paternal love and that higher spiritual state of which as yet he knows nothing.

Ought the teacher to be content with a mere mechanical recitation, or even with a faithful, interesting, intellectual discussion of the same?

Does his duty consist wholly or chiefly in imparting facts and scriptural knowledge to the young and inquiring mind? Will intellectual truths alone ever lead the soul to a true self-knowledge, to feel its weakness and sin, and its need of pardon through the Saviour?

Whatever may have been accomplished by such teaching, we feel more and more convinced that if any school possesses a vital, real, religious worth, efficiency, and power, it is just in proportion to the amount of true spiritual faith and life brought to bear upon the pupils by the individual teachers.

To awaken the spiritual life in another soul, to rouse the dormant affections and lead them to God, to persuade the spirit to feel its personal indebtedness to Christ as a Saviour, to kindle within it a deep sense of its need of divine renewal, and of pardon and salvation through a crucified Redeemer, — these are the highest, the noblest aims, such as are alone worthy the Christian teacher, and without which he ought never to assume such responsibilities.

The simple facts of Gospel truth are *comparatively* easy to teach, and here too many rest satisfied. Will such teaching be deemed sufficient in that hour when we are called upon in the Master's nearer presence to render up an account of the *souls* committed to our charge? No: there must first be in the heart the fire of devotion kindled from the secret altar, the realizing sense of divine things, the consciousness of addressing immortal spirits, if our words are to have any vital efficacy. Intellectual teaching, and the storing of the mind with religious facts and truths, is all-important in its place; but this *alone* never touches the heart, never calls forth the warm emotion, the grateful prayer, the repentant sigh. Soul must speak to soul. The child quickly and intuitively perceives when the whole heart is interested, and if this is wanting, truth, however divine, will fall cold and lifeless from his teacher's lips.

How many pupils are there who could relate accurately all the leading facts of the Gospel history! but is there a corresponding heart-knowledge, an interest in divine truths as a personal concern, vitally affecting the whole immortal being and destiny? And to how many in our schools, and in our churches, alas! is Christ only a dim, unreal abstraction of the Bible, with no reality and no vital power! Why is it that comparatively few, as they leave our schools, especially young men, take any active part in the support of religious institutions, or feel any strong attachment to the Church; — and that, during the very season of life when the soul most needs divine support and guidance, the feelings of self-reliance and self-confidence are so prevalent and strong?

Whatever may have been the deficiencies of home education, is not the evil to be ascribed, in a great measure, to the instructions imparted in our Sabbath schools? Must not the young be led to a holier self-consecration, to a deeper sense of the vital importance of religious truth, to a quickening consciousness of the worth of the soul, if we would have them in after years living pillars of the Church of Christ? Must they not be led to accept of Jesus as their Saviour in early youth, if in maturer years the soul would lay its purest offering of consecration and gratitude on the sacred altar of commemoration?

This leads us to consider another defect in much of the teaching of the present day, and one which is most radical and vital. We refer to the manner in which, by many, Christ is presented to the mind of the child. He is taught to look upon this pure and holy being as one whose example he is to imitate, whose teachings he is to obey, whose benevolent and loving life he is to follow in his walk among men, — in a word, as his Teacher and Guide alone; but the idea of Christ as his Saviour, the knowledge of the weakness and sin of his own heart, of his individual need of regeneration and salvation, and hope of happiness through the sole mediation of Christ, — these are views by many wholly excluded in the religious instruction of the young.

The solemn words of Christ with regard to the resurrection of the evil as well as the good, his representations of the sufferings of the impenitent, and of the ruin and loss of the soul save through humble penitence and a living faith in him, are too often left in the background; while representations of God's mercy, and of the greatness and dignity of human nature, are regarded as alone sufficient for the regeneration of the soul. In such teachings, is not a grievous wrong done to the mind of the child? Are we not substituting a superficial, sentimental piety, for the brave, whole-souled, hearty consecration of the whole spirit?

Were the teacher aware of the doubt and mental trials he is preparing for his pupil in after years, if he be one of any brightness of intellect or quickness of moral perceptions, by such partial representations of the truths of the Gospel, we believe that, if unaccustomed to mental research or studious inquiry, he would pause and ponder, and consider with earnest thought the truth of his teachings in their whole bearing, ere writing them out in ineffaceable lines on the susceptible heart of childhood.

We need to have truths presented honestly and fairly; to have sin, of whatever form, called sin, in all its native deformity and evil; to have the inevitable suffering and punishment of sin solemnly and faithfully set forth; and the hope of pardon brought home to the soul, as dependent on the free mercy of God revealed in Christ, as the only Saviour of men. We need to have the necessity of the new birth, — of the conversion and regeneration of the soul from sin to holiness, — taught as an essential truth of the Gospel to every individual, and not to let the abundant mercy and goodness of God be so abused as to leave out of sight his equally divine attributes of holiness and justice; but, through the clear, full representation of these, to have the soul led to him, through Christ as the Saviour who can redeem it from the power of sin; as the Saviour who gives the assurance of future happiness and eternal life to the regenerate spirit as indeed the very gift of God, — Christ, the power of God and the wisdom of God; the only name under heaven, given among men, whereby we can be saved.

"'Thou must be born again!'
Such was the solemn word
To him who came, not all in vain,
By night to seek his Lord.

"'Thou must be born again!'
But not the birth of clay;
The immortal seed must thence obtain
Deliverance unto day.

"Thou canst not choose but trace
The steps thy Master trod,
If once thou feel his truth and grace,
A conscious child of God."

Feeling this truth, and conscious of the divine help and blessing, let the teacher go to his work in the spirit of faith and of prayer. Let him converse judiciously, yet freely, with his pupils on their *personal* religious concerns, teaching them the necessity of a new birth, of their weakness and helplessness without divine aid, of the certainty of a righteous retribution, and thus leading them to Christ as a personal Saviour. Let him teach them, through his own life-giving spirit, that, however young, *they* have a part in the promises and hopes of the Gospel; and never let him rest satisfied with listening merely to a recitation, or teaching *mere* facts. Such a Sabbath hour, if not lost, is far, very far, from accomplishing its highest end.

Immortal spirits are before you, — spirits with earnest aspirations, longing desires, strong passions, and warm affections, — spirits capable of rising to an archangel's glory, or of sinking into degradation, misery, and spiritual death.

Have you no direct, earnest message to such? No word of personal appeal, of gentle sympathy and encouragement, or of solemn warning? Living now in eternity, with the solemnities of being for ever encompassing you, must your lips be sealed upon the most momentous of all themes, those which directly affect the eternal, immortal destiny of those under your care?

How much might be gained by this free communion of soul with soul, especially among the older pupils! It is no longer the sometimes cold and mere mechanical relation of teacher and pupil, but immortal spirits pressing on to the same heavenly goal!

Pressingly and deeply do we need in all our schools the life of religious sensibility, a faith that trusts in God, a realizing sense of dependence on the Saviour, a felt reality in things invisible. We need to have truths brought home to the heart, baptized in the living light of the Gospel, sanctified by the influences of the Spirit. The mere outward form of the lesson, important as it is, sinks into comparative insignificance, when this one great end of all religious teaching is inwardly recognized, — to labor for the regeneration and salvation of immortal souls.

Such aims, and such alone, are worthy of our Sabbath schools, or of any mode of religious teaching; and such alone, kept steadily and constantly in view, will render them efficient means of usefulness, — schools of a noble, true, and elevated Christian nurture.

In the deeply interesting memoir of the late Dr. Judson, — that devoted missionary of the cross, whose labors, sufferings, and entire self-consecration to his Master's service have given him a name worthy to be ranked among the noblest and most faithful of the followers of Christ in any age, — we find the following passage, which affords a key to the secret of his ultimate success and influence, whether among Burmans, Karens, or Hindoos.

"He always kept one object steadily in view, to the exclusion of every other. It was, not to teach men a creed, or to train them to the performance of certain rites, or to persuade them to belong to a particular church, but, first of all, to produce in them a radical change of moral character, to lead them to repent of and forsake all sin, to love God with an affection that should transcend in power every other motive, and to rely for salvation on faith in Christ. . . . . . It was by embracing every opportunity which his intercourse with men presented to tell them of the love of Christ, of their danger and their duty, and to urge them, in Christ's stead, to be reconciled to God."

Keeping this one aim distinctly in view, devoting to it the whole energy of a strong and controlling will, pursuing it with indomitable fixedness of purpose, never allowing himself to be turned aside by any temptations to ease, by the most fearful personal suffering, or even by the allurements of society or literary enjoyment, resolutely, firmly, and prayerfully he pursued this high calling, — to reclaim the ignorant and the wandering, and to make known to them the unsearchable riches of Christ.

Is it said that these representations of the true

aim and object of Sunday-school instruction as have here been given present a standard altogether too high, and such as would repel many who might otherwise be induced to enter into its labors? Far indeed be it from us to say anything, here or anywhere, that would repel one true desire, discourage one sincere purpose, or repress one single effort to do good in any form. "He that is not against us is for us," were the words of the one chief Shepherd; but he also added, "He that gathereth not with me, scattereth abroad." We do not believe that a determinate aim and a lofty standard, to any brave, resolute, aspiring soul, will ever prove discouraging. There is always something fascinating, as well as noble and Christian, in keeping such a standard in view. A true knowledge of the deepest wants, as well as of the highest aspirations, of the human soul is revealed in those words of the Saviour: "Be ye perfect, even as your Father in heaven is perfect."

> "We cannot be too rich in faith,
> We cannot be too strong of wing;
> Thyself, — thyself thou offerest
> To our sublime endeavoring."

What but such an aim, and such a lofty standard, and such a working faith, sustained the glowing enthusiasm and earnestness of Paul, leading him to brave undauntedly persecution, suffering, and death, the scoffs of rulers and the indignities of the multitude, so that he might win souls to Christ? What but this can sustain the heart and quicken the faithful zeal of any true Christian teacher, however humble his duties may seem to the world's eye?

Give us this, and other defects will soon be remedied. Give us this, and there will be vitality and power where now there is deadness and indifference. Give us such aims, such a spirit, such a life, in any school, or any band of teachers,—nay, in any one teacher,—and it will tell on the open and yielding heart of childhood, "with a benignity of influence, of such holy and regenerative power, as no reach of vision, save that prophetic eye that looks into the immortal ages, can measure."

CHAPTER IV.

QUALIFICATIONS OF THE TEACHER. — FAITH IN CHRIST AND SELF-CONSECRATION.

"A living faith in Christ implies an immediate, conscious, personal relation."

"Our blest Redeemer, ere he breathed
His tender, last farewell,
A Guide, a Comforter bequeathed
With us to dwell.

"He came sweet influence to impart,
A gracious, willing guest,
While he can find one humble heart
Wherein to rest.

"And every virtue we possess,
And every victory won,
And every thought of holiness,
Are his alone."

Having spoken of the true and definite aim which every teacher should keep constantly in view, the question naturally suggests itself, "Who are fitted to fill this office? What qualifications are essential to form a successful teacher of religious truths? Are high attainments and a mature religious experience necessary, ere one assumes this office? What personal traits of character are requisite to render one a true and faithful guide to the young and inexperienced?"

We would answer, in general terms, that but one thing is absolutely essential, for where this exists, all else will follow naturally and in its due time; namely, *the self-consecration of the soul to God through Christ.* Let there only be this one purpose, this one sincere desire, to love and obey God, to follow Christ in heart and in life, to be his earnest, true, and faithful disciple, and however young, however inexperienced, the soul thus consecrated cannot but exert a power that will diffuse its own silent and secret influence over other spirits. It may make no pretensions, utter no formal words of piety, never intrude its convictions at unseasonable times or places, but its power will be felt and known. It can no more conceal the true source of its hidden life and light than the sun can hide its beams at noonday. It may imagine its own sphere too narrow and too limited to attract any notice from others, or it may go on in the regular and faithful performance of daily duty, and, like Mrs. Ware, be all unmindful of the mighty influence exerted over thousands of other souls, so quietly, so unconsciously, and yet so trustingly, had the work been wrought. The power is *there*, the attraction which binds the soul to Christ is *felt*, and where more readily than by the loving heart of childhood? *We* may see the thousand imperfections of others, we may doubt the efficacy of their teachings and question their influence, but if the *love of Christ* be in the soul a potent spring of action, if its *ruling desire* be to manifest its heart-felt gratitude by a life of obedience, if its prevailing purpose be to draw nearer and nearer in a heart-union with Him, that desire and that purpose will touch the hearts of the young and untried, and will kindle holier feelings, and purer affections, and warmer aspirations. The Saviour sent forth his early Apostles to labor in his vineyard, not as those who were perfect in spirit, but as those who *loved him* above all human friends, and were ready to relinquish all to do his will. When we witness the mighty influence of their simple and earnest appeals, when we hear them speaking as with tongues of fire, and see the thousands converted in a single day, — when we see them bravely and undauntedly confronting persecution, ignominy, and death, that they might win souls to Christ, distrusting their own strength, yet strong in the power of the Omnipotent, — we feel that there was a hidden source of power, a secret spring of influence, which ever acted upon their souls, quickening, purifying, and elevating; a love, deep, fervent, and unquenchable, to their divine Master.

Is it said, that this alone can never render one

an effective teacher of others? Feel this inward attraction in your own heart, — know from personal experience the secret guidance and influence of the Spirit, — and then give the only true answer.

"O, hope of every contrite heart!
O, joy of all the meek!
To those who fall how kind thou art!
How good to those who seek!

"But what to those who find? Ah, this
Nor tongue nor pen can show!
The love of Jesus, what it is
None but his loved ones know."

How beautiful and powerful are the influences flowing from such a principle of action! Look at the gentle and loving Schwartz,* whose life was passed on the distant plains of India, amid a stranger nation, a pioneer in the great cause of Eastern missions; often surrounded by danger and exposed to peril and suffering, but whose faith never faltered, and whose zeal never abated, even when the snows of threescore years and ten encircled his brow as with a crown of glory. "His life, a beautiful copy of that of his Redeemer, spoke to the heart of the Hindoo with a calm, yet resistless, conviction. During the first years that he came among them, they lis-

* Christian Frederic Schwartz, born at Sonnenburg, Germany, October 26, 1726; died at Tanjore, India, September, 1797.

tened coldly and curiously to his teachings. It was not till they were surprised and charmed with the integrity and purity of his character that the doctrines he taught met with any success. A corrupt, licentious, and subtile people, who could not discern, among all the priests and professors of their religion, a single example of true virtue, self-denial, or devotedness, they looked on this man, inflamed with love and zeal, seduced neither by the power nor the bribes of princes, turning from the palace to each humble home, to mourn, to rejoice, to pray, — they looked, and at last believed." Deeply imbued with his Master's love and sympathy, forbearance, and tender condescension, — this was the true secret of his power. "He spoke gently and pleadingly, but it was an earnest and all-impressive gentleness, that sank into the soul, as the low, sweet tones of heart-felt music will touch the inmost depths of the spirit far sooner than the most artistic symphonies." It has been well said, that "no man ever succeeded greatly in a career in which he did not feel a delight, even to enthusiasm." With Schwartz, this interest and enthusiasm were sustained by a divine power and love, and never abated, even to the last failing energy of life. When, at a good old age, he peacefully passed from earth, to wider and nobler spheres of duty, many were the tears of true affection shed over his mortal remains, by those whom he had befriended; — the orphan children for whom he had evinced a father's care and tenderness; the prince whose rightful claims he had firmly upheld; those of noble caste and extended influence, as well as the poor, desolate, and forsaken, whom he had turned from the darkness of superstition, ignorance, and idolatry, to the only true light and life. A beautiful monument to his memory, wrought by the graceful genius of Flaxman, now adorns the Christian church at Tanjore, but a more enduring monument than one of marble is the memory of his Christ-like life and pure example; while the seed of truth, sown by him in weakness, yet with a living faith, has sprung up and borne fruit, even a hundredfold, — fulfilling his own words of holy trust, uttered when every prospect of success seemed dark and dreary, — "Perhaps the fruit will appear when I am laid at rest."

> "Soldier of Christ, well done!
> Praise be thy blest employ;
> And while eternal ages run,
> Rest in thy Saviour's joy!"

Truly has it been said, "The heart's affections originate and *compel* work. The heart wrought upon, and then given, an inexhaustible fountain is opened, out of which all spiritual action must proceed."

This personal sense of indebtedness to Christ, this union of the soul with him, can alone render one a true and effective teacher, — for this alone can impart life, — and life we need; not dull indifference, not mere commonplaces of piety, not a tame mediocrity, that may seem well enough to the world's eye, but a life pregnant with force, drawing its inspiration from the hidden counsels of divine wisdom, sustaining its strength by resting on the eternal words of promise. Life, — not coldness, not indifference, but life, however manifested, however varied, if so be that it is true and earnest; — even that secret life which is hid with Christ in God.

Have we such a life in our schools? — and if so, why are not more definite and permanent results manifested? What is the true meaning of such self-consecration? Do we not too often belittle its force, and seek to fashion it according to our own low aims and worldly standard of attainment?

First and chief of all, it implies a sense of individual want and weakness, and a reliance on the free and unmerited mercy of God revealed through Christ; a sense of personal union with the Saviour, and of indebtedness to him as the soul's only refuge and strength. It is more than an intellectual faith in the teachings of Christ, more than a general feeling of the worth and importance of Gospel truth and a vague desire to lead a Christian life; more than a mere impulse of goodness and a wish to follow a certain fashion of benevolence. It is the giving up of the soul to God; it is the secret confession breathed in the words of lowly and penitent prayer; it is the yielding up, once and for ever, all sense or claim of personal merit, and relying on the Spirit for guidance, help, and direction.

Can a teacher speak of these divine truths, unless he has felt their power in his own soul? unless he has experienced his own deep need of a Saviour, and felt the powerful influence of the cross? Is there not among us too much of a mere intellectual knowledge of Christ, as God's chosen Messiah, derived from reading or education, without a vital heart-union with him? Is there a living faith in the peculiar influences of the Holy Spirit, as derived *through* Christ, and dependent on him as the ever-present mediator? In how many minds, indeed, is there a mere vague, general belief in the agency and influence of the Spirit, consisting of little more than the soothing influences often derived from the contemplation of some beautiful scene in nature or some master-work of art; from the calmness of the early morning, or the often richer glories of the sunset hour; dependent, perchance, upon the tranquil state of the nerves, or the quietness and success of the outward life! And with such, how little depth of meaning is attached to expressions like these, "being baptized with the Holy Spirit, being *filled*, *renewed*, *sanctified* by the Spirit"!

Without this sense of union with the Saviour, without this conscious guidance of the Spirit, can any soul truly guide, direct, and aid another soul in its heavenward course?

High attainments, or a *mature* faith, are not essential; but some spiritual, realizing consciousness of the true relation of the soul to God and to Christ *is* essential.

By many teachers is Christ thus presented to the child? Is he led to feel that the Saviour is ever present with him, sympathizing in his joys and trials, watching his progress, strengthening each better endeavor, interested in every little conquest and every true effort? Is he taught to pray through Christ for the divine blessing, receiving each spiritual gift through him as the one Mediator, looking to him as his final Judge, as the Reconciler of the soul to God? In fine, is the image of Jesus so blended with the instructions and impressions received, that it becomes, even in childhood, a reality to the soul?

We complain of and deplore the result; but does not the evil lie deeper than many imagine, even in the child's earliest education, in those years when impressions are the strongest, and the affections the warmest and most vital, and when too often the young spirit is left to itself to gain its first religious impressions, at mere hazard, from any chance seed that may be sown in the open soil? How often, *too*, even in the

Christian household, is mere *general* religious instruction and influence imparted, and no direct parental efforts made to become acquainted with the peculiar wants, workings, trials, and questionings of the child's heart! Where there is any natural diffidence or reserve, especially in speaking of the deeper cravings and wants of the spirit, this only increases and strengthens as years pass on, until the hour of anxious self-questioning arises, when happy for the spirit if it find some Christian friend or teacher, in whose experience it can confide, and receive the help and guidance and sympathy it needs!

Oh! were those who have the care and guidance of the young, in any degree aware of the deep impressions made in early childhood; of the difficulty of building up this living, realizing faith in after years, when it has not been interwoven in the very fabric of the child's heart, we believe that many would pause ere taking upon themselves the sacred responsibilities of teacher or guide, and first ask in deep self-scrutiny, "Have I a living faith in Christ? Do I feel my personal relationship to him? Do I so love the Saviour, through a consciousness of what he has done for my own soul, as to speak in sincerity to the young spirit of that divine love, and to strive to lead it in early life to the fold of the Redeemer? Have I a practical faith in the quickening, sustaining, sanctifying influences of the Holy Spirit, and is it my daily prayer that my whole soul may be baptized with its divine power?

A mere intellectual faith, a belief in Christ as a holy teacher alone, as the Messiah of the past, may be sufficient to some minds; but it serves not the soul in the hour of deep self-questioning, when the surging waves of conscience and memory rise in their gigantic force, and the holiness of God, and his perfect law, stand a vivid reality before the soul, disclosing all its secret and hidden depths; it serves not in those silent watches of the night-season, or in those hours of physical prostration, when the darkened chamber, the hushed whisper, and the gentle footstep leave the soul to its own self-communings, and the thought arises in its solemn power,

> "Thou must go forth alone, my soul!
> Thou must go forth alone,
> To other scenes, to other worlds,
> That mortal hath not known.
> Alone must thou go forth, my soul,
> To meet thy God above!"

It serves not amid the daily duties and toils of life, the cares, anxieties, and perplexities, the joys and griefs of each passing hour, when the soul needs a more than human helper to sustain its composure, to preserve its rectitude, to quench the rising passion, to impart peace.

Are we told that Christ came to introduce and establish a new system of religion, and that through his perfect moral teachings alone the human mind is to develop and educate itself? Are we taught that a faithful, conscientious performance of *duty* is all that God or the Gospel requires; and that such a life brings its own reward, here and hereafter? Point us, we would reply, to any one heart that in this way *alone* has found true strength, or the deepest peace, and we will surrender our own views. No: a living Saviour does the soul need; a sense of the personal sympathy, the ever-quickening influence of a present Christ; to feel even *now* the thrilling touch of the Master's hand, and, like the disciple of old, trustingly to repose on his breast.

Tell us not only of the dignity of human nature, for self-knowledge utters its cry of inward want, failure, and destitution; tell us not alone of the innate capacities of the soul and its power of self-development, for vain mockeries are they to the soul in its hours of deepest need; tell us not of the goodness of God as revealed in the beautiful harmony of the outward universe alone, as if this were an all-sufficient anchor to the spirit; for there are moments when the cloud within casts its dark shadow over the fairest scenes and the brightest skies, and faint and uncertain is nature's response to the earnest questionings of the spirit.

There are periods in the lives of all when ab stract truths lose their power. In those seasons when the waves and billows of adversity sweep over the soul, when all outward supports fail, and even the tenderest human sympathy seems cold and vain to the desolate and bleeding heart; when sudden and desolating grief bows the spirit in bitter anguish, and the joy of peaceful days is swept away in a moment, — the soul turns not to arguments, nor to intellectual truths, nor to any mere *words* of revelation, for such are then all too cold and lifeless. It turns to *Christ:* it seeks his consoling presence; the tender sympathy that wept with the mourning sisters at the grave of Lazarus, and uttered those soothing words of peace to the trembling and sorrowing disciples, "Let not your heart be troubled; my peace I give unto you." It follows him to the garden-shades, and learns from that bitter agony of the love made perfect through suffering; and as it bends at the foot of the cross, and there reads the lesson of sublime self-renunciation, and of love, stronger than death, it feels and believes, that, even though the furnace be seven times heated, One is ever with it who will bring it forth unharmed. It knows that the ministering angels of God's love are near, and it believes and trusts; for He who dwells in the bosom of the Father is with it, giving the needed strength, and abiding with it as the ever-present Comforter.

No: abstract truths, moral formulas, however pure and sublime, have little power to touch the heart, to kindle heavenly aspirations, to awaken the dormant sensibilities. It was something far more and deeper than these that has led the noble army of apostles, martyrs, and missionaries to yield up all for Christ. It was more than these that induced Martyn, in the vigor of opening manhood, to give up home, and friends, and country, to relinquish the rich emoluments of talent and industry, to lay down his life on the burning plains of the East, amid a strange and heathen nation, — an early and a noble sacrifice. It was more than cold abstractions that sustained the tender love and untiring zeal of Brainerd and Eliot, as they proclaimed the words of Gospel truth amid the deep wilds of American forests; that led the gentle Mrs. Boardman to seek the shores of India, leaving all that woman's heart holds so dear, and nobly and undauntedly to meet the privations and toils of years of suffering, sustained by a power not her own; that led Oberlin to make his home amid the snow-crowned Alps, and Howard to close his faithful years, laboring to alleviate the horrors of dungeons and prisons. It was no formal utterance of abstract truths, or of an intellectual faith alone, that gathered crowds to hear the loving words of Cheverus, that breathed in the tender, winning accents of Fénelon, that moved and swayed the breathless multitude as they listened to the soul-stirring words of Edwards, or to the moving eloquence of Whitefield and Wesley.

It was no cold and formal truths that led the little band of Moravian missionaries to the bleak and barren shores of Greenland, that enabled them to labor amid hardships and discouragements such as would have wholly deterred hearts less earnest and trusting, and that enabled them to speak with such persuasive fervor and zeal that the hearts of the ignorant and degraded were melted and touched, as they proclaimed the divine message of pardon and salvation.

No: they spoke of *Christ.* They pointed to that central figure, the embodiment of all truth and power, and love and wisdom, and bade the sinful, the ignorant, and the dying turn to him as their only refuge and support. They felt his presence and his love in their own souls, and so their words were redolent with power, and their tongues kindled as with the fire of inspiration.

Teach, then, the child of *Christ the Saviour,* and of the Father of perfect holiness and love, manifested in and through him. Let soul speak to soul; and though the teacher may possess no peculiar talent, no high attainments, this inward power and principle will be felt. Let his daily and fervent prayer be, to be brought into a conscious union with his divine Master, to *abide in him*, as the branch in the vine, and to feel that all his life is derived from the Father through him.

Such teachers are needed in our schools,— souls *consecrated to Christ*, feeling that the Gospel is addressed to them individually, and that they have a solemn responsibility in proclaiming its words of divine truth.

A consciousness of imperfection and sin will not deter them from the work, for they will feel that He who spake the words of pardon and of peace to the weeping woman that bathed his feet in tears of humble penitence, will not reject any soul that clings to him in tender love, and seeks to follow him in daily duty. Of the humbled Publican, not of the self-complacent Pharisee, was it said, that "he went down to his house justified."

Let us have this life of Christ in our schools, this inward, spiritual love of the Saviour, filling the hearts of the teachers, and life will spring from barrenness, and verdure and bloom will cover every waste and desert place, and the promise of the Father will come upon each waiting soul, through his Christ, — even the baptism of the Holy Spirit.

CHAPTER V.

QUALIFICATIONS OF THE TEACHER. — INTEREST AND PERSEVERANCE IN THE WORK, AND A TRUE LOVE OF SOULS.

"Take heed unto thyself. . . . . Study to show thyself approved unto God, a workman that needeth not to be ashamed, rightly dividing the word of truth. . . . . And the servant of the Lord must not strive; but be gentle unto all men, apt to teach, patient."

"I INTEND to take a class in your Sabbath school," said a young lady to a friend who for several years had been engaged as teacher; "and I want your assistance in engaging some pupils, for I know of but one at present whom I can persuade to come." The required promise was readily given, and in the course of another week the young lady was informed that three little children were ready to enter the school for the first time, taken from homes of poverty and ignorance, having enjoyed no religious instruction, and especially needing the kind and simple lessons of love and of truth that she might be able to impart. "O I do not want such a class as that," was the quick rejoinder; "I had rather wait till I can find some children more inviting to teach; I never could do anything with such as those, I am sure, they are so uninteresting." And so the golden opportunity was lost, and another and a truer disciple of her Master was found, to unseal the fountains of spiritual truth to those young and thirsting souls, one to whom it shall be said hereafter, "Inasmuch as ye did it unto one of the least of these, ye did it unto me."

Could such a spirit as was here exhibited have been calculated to exert a beneficial influence over the young and inexperienced? Was there any true self-consecration to the Master's service? any realizing sense of the worth of the soul, and of the Father's love for the youngest and the feeblest spirit? Are there no such teachers now in any of our schools? Is there not among *us* too much of the spirit of ease and self-indulgence, and too little of the true missionary spirit of self-renunciation, of that deep *love* of our work which would lead us to count all things as naught, so that we might win souls to Christ?

If the teacher enter upon his office simply as a matter of course, because he is anxious to follow others, or merely to pass a Sabbath hour agreeably among five or six well-behaved, well-dressed children, making little or no preparation for his duties beforehand, and deeming those duties fulfilled when the appointed lesson is well recited, though but a portion of the time allotted to such recitations be thus occupied, what ought to be expected? what is the necessary and real result? As we sow, so shall we reap. Indifference, or a superficial goodness, or a faith merely founded upon the intellect, and having no deep, abiding root in the soul, must be the natural consequence of such teaching. Where a teacher undertakes his responsible office, virtually expressing, in so doing, his faith in Christ as his own guide and example, and his desire so to follow his life of benevolence and self-sacrifice as to be the means of leading young hearts to choose him as their only teacher and guide, of bringing back the lost and wandering to look to him as their only sufficient Saviour and Redeemer, and yet is unwilling to take under his charge any but the well-dressed children of the more favored classes among us, is there not some vital defect in his spirit, which, if he has any true self-knowledge, ought to deter him from taking such an office at all? Can he possess that love of souls which alone can render his teaching effective?

We well know the discouragements attending the charge of a class of the more ignorant and neglected children among us; but we know, too, the happiness and the good resulting from such intercourse; and we cannot but feel, that in most instances where no good has been effected, the want of success is to be attributed in part to the teacher, as well as to adverse home influences We have known instances where a teacher has had children for months under his care, who yet has never seen them in their own homes; never expressed any interest in the long sickness of a parent, brother, or sister; never testified that in any way they were associated with other than the Sabbath hours. We have known other teachers, who have seen the neglect, undertake the offices of Christian charity to such children, in addition to those under their immediate care, speaking the kindly word of sympathy at home, and creating ties of spiritual love and gratitude, which the nominal teacher in vain could expect to form. When the former have complained of coldness or indifference, or want of success, and have wondered how others possessed the "tact" of interesting such ignorant and uneducated minds, we have sometimes thought that the true cause was sought everywhere but within. Are the discouragements attending the instruction of such children more or greater than must be encountered by every true teacher in the charge of those who come from mere worldly and fashionable homes, where the voice of prayer is seldom or never heard, and the Bible is regarded as only a book for Sundays, or its gilded covers as a suitable ornament for the centre-table? Has not the teacher even a more difficult work here to perform in overcoming frivolity and indifference, and in breaking through the hard crust of self-satisfied complacency and self-righteousness? If the child or youth sees the teacher, who speaks to him in the Sabbath hours of the duties of self-denial and self-consecration, of the supreme importance of eternal realities, and of the comparative worthlessness and insignificance of the merely external and outward, absorbed during the week in every passing pleasure, — devoted to dress and fashion and gain, fond of flattery and amusement, making no systematic or earnest efforts for self-improvement or the good of others, — what wonder that he regards the instructions of the Seventh day as of little worth or importance! No: the work is regarded as far too *easy* a one, and so, too often, those of little spiritual energy, vital religious power, or practical force of character, enter into the labor, expecting to reap at once an abundant harvest, and are disappointed because they only reap as they have sown. The eye of the child is quick and ready to discern; and unless there be in the teacher a true and heart-felt love, and a spirit of patient, calm perseverance in his work, in vain will it be to address to the pupil mere words of goodness; he will see through the shallow artifice, and his own languid interest will but reflect the teacher's spirit.

A truer self-consecration and a more genuine vital energy are needed among us. Something of that resolute zeal by which Chalmers effected so much amid the crowded streets and narrow lanes of Glasgow, in bringing the neglected children of want and ignorance under the influence of well-regulated schools and faithful teachers, and which led him to say, in deep earnestness, to those engaged with him in the same noble work "Until men go forth among our heathen at home with the same zeal and enthusiasm which are expected of missionaries who go abroad, there will be little true knowledge of religion throughout the mass of our city families, or a reclaiming of them from those sad habits of alienation from God and from goodness into which the vast majority of them have fallen."

We want, not only those who are ready to labor beneath sunny skies and in a serene atmosphere, where a quiet, simple routine is to be weekly passed through, and no difficulties encountered, no opposition experienced; but we need spirits made strong through endurance, resolute by action, stringent by earnest exercise. In this cause, if in any, we need the energy and zeal manifested in other departments of duty, amid the routine of business, the competition for distinction, the struggle for literary eminence and fame. Let the teacher go to his duties with heart and mind, energy and strength. Listlessness and indifference are the sure forerunners of spiritual death.

Let him be *awake* to his work. Spiritual indolence is a most subtle enemy, and one more to be feared by every true-hearted Christian than any other. Where there is a Christ-like, living spirit, "it will never suffer the individual to sit idly with folded hands, looking lazily out on the white fields of harvest, where no reaper's sickle rings against the wheat; but it will send him forth to work, nerved with an impulse that no disappointment can palsy, no misgivings keep back." Such an energy, not fitful and spasmodic, but having its seat in the inmost soul, cannot but be effectual and life-giving.

In the Christian teacher, one of its first and most essential fruits will manifest itself by a faithful *punctuality* in all the duties of his office. His seat will not be found vacant every time that the weather is a little unpropitious, or any little personal effort is needed for him to be present at the appointed hour; but he will regard it as an essential duty to the whole school, no less than to his individual class, to be at his post regularly and punctually, unless sickness or absolute necessity detains him from his duties.

Nothing can be more injurious to the discipline and regularity of a school, than to have the baneful example of teachers who are inconstant in their attendance, or who, by a late and hurried entrance, interrupt the opening exercises of the school. Order, regularity, and method are *essen-*

tial to every well-arranged and well-governed school, and these ends cannot be secured without the co-operation of the individual teacher. At the cost of whatever personal effort, let him feel that there is an absolute obligation laid upon him so to act; for as regularly and punctually should he be at his post as the teacher of any of our secular schools.

If he is obliged to be absent, or to suspend his duties for a season, let him give due notice to the superintendent, and make such arrangements as may be possible to have his place supplied. Nothing is more discouraging to a class, and more surely quenches at once all ardor and interest in their pursuits, than to go Sunday after Sunday, and find their teacher absent; or if they are in season, to have him enter, when the opening exercises have been performed, or the school is half over. Every teacher should be in his place *before* the opening of the school, and be ready in a calm, quiet, and collected spirit, to meet his pupils.

A faithful and eminently successful teacher, now passed from earth, always made it his practice to be in his seat some minutes before his pupils, in order to find time to collect his thoughts, to offer renewedly the secret prayer for guidance and a special blessing on his instructions, and to realize more fully his Master's presence and sympathy in his immediate labors. Might not such a practice be beneficial to every teacher? and still more, would not its spirit react with vital power upon every pupil?

If these duties are undertaken in the spirit of Christ, with a sincere desire to be a minister of good to other souls, there must also exist in the teacher's heart the Saviour's spirit of self-renunciation, of patient love and sympathy. To speak to the heart of the child, we must understand something of its wants and desires, its joys and griefs, its hopes and fears. We must *feel* with him, make his individual character a close study, and regard nothing as little that contributes to his happiness, or that ever brings a shadow over his youthful brow. What seem little things to us, trials and joys too trivial to mention, are great to him; and it is in and through these daily and seemingly trivial events that he is to be led to a true self-conquest, and a trusting, child-like faith.

Tell him not in abstract terms of love and duty and immortality; but touch those warm and glowing affections, too often repressed by ignorance, or sin, or coldness; lead him to confide in you as a loving, sympathizing friend, to whom he may freely trust his troubles and his joys, — then bring before him that Holy One, who took the little children in his arms and blessed them, who rolled back the shadow of death from the brow of the young Jewish maiden, and who himself became the child of sorrow and of suffering, *that for evermore its power might be transfigured to human hearts.*

Tell him of the kind and good Father who watches over him, and loves him, and cares for him infinitely more than the best of earthly parents; associate the thought of God with all that is glad and beautiful in life; teach him to look above for a blessing, with the brightness of each opening morning, and to seek the shelter of the same watchful care and love, as the evening shades gather around his home.

Let no coldness, no sternness, no unsympathizing word or look repress the childish utterance of love, or chill the warm glow of his young affections. Let him not feel that the religion of Jesus has no part in the joys of childhood, or the gladness of opening youth, but through a cheerful faith, a ready sympathy, and a glad participation in all that contributes to his innocent amusement or true improvement, let him learn the *reality* and the *joy* of a true religious faith and hope.

Some there are well fitted for their vocation in all but this, — they do not enter into the child's feelings, nor learn through a gentle sympathy the access to his heart. It is like an unknown region to them. " Father," said a bright, intelligent boy of nine years, as the hour for school arrived; "Father, if you will let me be in Mr. B.'s class, I should like to go; but if not, I do not want to attend school any longer, for I do n't think my teacher cares anything about me. He hears and explains my lessons, it is true, but I know he do n't love me." And yet there was no more conscientious and intelligent teacher in the school than the one referred to but he had studied truth too much in reference to the intellect only, and realized not the essential importance of studying even more the child's heart, and of learning how to enter into his active, inquisitive mind.

The heart *must* breathe in the words and manner. Teach the child in every possible way, by every little attention, every word of encouragement or admonition, that yours is a deep and a true interest, and your instructions will not be in vain. Expect not to mark the same interest, or to witness the same results in all, but study each individual character, and seek to bring out the peculiar excellencies of each; to learn their different tastes, habits, and feelings. Show that you appreciate their least endeavors; for a word of encouragement will often do far more than reproof. If the child be indolent and careless, seek worthy stimulants to rouse him to exertion; if cold and indifferent, strive to quicken his dormant affections; if irritable and petulant, evince always a quiet and firm manner, and teach him by your own gentle and loving spirit the beauty of a Christ-like temper. Never reprove in harshness, or before others, wounding the delicate sensitiveness of the child's heart. Talk not of his peculiar faults before the whole class, but speak to him alone or in private, and expose not his susceptible feelings to the laugh or gaze of others. Lead him to feel that you have confidence in his power of improvement, and so awaken in him a true self-reliance; for constant fault-finding is always and everywhere depressing. Never reprove or admonish when there is the least degree of anger or impatience in your own soul. A reproof loses all its moral majesty and its due effect when the tongue teaches one thing, and the manner, voice, and expression of countenance wholly another.

Insist on order and obedience in your class from the very first, for nothing can be accomplished without these. Be firm, dignified, and resolute, and at the same time gentle and affectionate.

Let not any pupil receive a partial attention. Turn not to the bright, intelligent, and thoughtful, as if they were to receive exclusive care; but remember, that beneath the coarse garb, uninteresting exterior, and often repulsive bearing of the child of ignorance and want, there are the germs of a life as true and noble as in the more favored child of affluence and of joy. Nay: give a double attention to such, — show them a deeper love and a more tender sympathy, for they need it more. It may, indeed, be more pleasant to train the delicate and cultivated plant, and watch its beautiful unfolding; but the rough and unsightly shrub will often yield the richest and most abundant fruit, — and "by their *fruits* ye shall know them."

May it not be, that your love, your simple words of kindness, alone stand between the child and a cold, unsympathizing world? Home he may know only as a nightly shelter, — perchance not even that; and a parent's name brings up no endearing thought, recalls no soothing, gentle voice of love. You may imagine your endeavors all fruitless and void; but in after years it may be that your image will blend with those loving words, "Our Father," and he will bless God for one who shed a single beam of light upon his benighted and darkened childhood. Would not such a consciousness be an ample reward for every sacrifice and discouragement?

Stand, for once, beside the dying bed of such a child; all is cheerless in the cold and desolate room; no mother's gentle voice speaks of the good Shepherd's care, or soothes the weary spirit, as it passes through the dark valley; no cheering words of faith and hope point the departing soul to the glad, bright home above; but noisy words and harsh discords fall on the ear, with no loving hand to bathe the aching brow or soothe the weary limbs. But amid all the noisy strife and all the outward cheerlessness, see how the little hand clasps the simple hymn-book given her by her teacher one glad summer's morning, and which brought so bright a smile over the careworn face, as she was told that it was "her own"; listen to the half-murmured words of the last Sabbath lesson, —

"'Let little children come to me,'
The blessed Saviour said";

watch the bright smile that steals over the pallid face, and beams in heavenly beauty amid such a scene, as if the Saviour were indeed visibly present to that young spirit, waiting to receive it to his arms of love; and then turn away, and ask, if you can, "Is it a light thing to be a teacher to such as these?"

Not many months since, a young man in a sailor's garb entered the store of a merchant in the city of P——. On being asked what he wished for, as he carelessly leaned over the counter, he looked steadily into the merchant's face, and in a trembling voice exclaimed, "Do you not know William H——, your old pupil?" Well might he ask the question, for his whole exterior was not more changed than the expression of his countenance, once cold, careless, and indifferent, now full of life and animation, and speaking of a conscience no longer silenced and disobeyed.

In relating to his friend his personal adventures as a sailor, during the previous five years, he made the following touching remarks: —

"I well know the trouble I gave you, when in your class at Sunday school; how utterly heedless I was of all your instructions, and how in every way I tried to thwart your endeavors. One Sunday, in company with H——, I behaved even worse than usual, and you told me that you should be obliged to dismiss me from the school, unless I would promise to behave better. You talked seriously and very earnestly to me. I felt it all, but was too proud to show it, and I determined to brave it out, though in my heart I knew you were my best friend.

"However, the next week, being somewhat ashamed and weary of my vagrant kind of life, and dreading too, more than all, my mother's quiet reproof, I engaged as a sailor on board the merchant ship 'Columbus.'

"The next Sunday morning, I thought I would just go into school once more, as I really felt a little homesick at the thought of going to sea for the first time, to be absent many months. The opening hymn was being sung, as I noisily entered. I took my seat, but cared, as usual, little for the lessons. Had you spoken coldly or harshly, it would have been all over with me. But when you took my hand so kindly, and spoke so earnestly, pleading with me to leave off my bad habits, I felt more ashamed, more self-convicted, than ever before. I said nothing; but when you bade me 'good by,' using no reproachful words, and the next morning went all the way to the wharf to see me safe on board the vessel, and placed this very Bible in my hands, I could no longer resist your patient kindness. Often and often did your words come back to me amid the busy scenes of the day, or when watching alone by night on the cold deck, and I then solemnly determined, God helping me, to lead a better life.

"Months and years have passed, but you have never been forgotten in my daily prayers; and I determined, if ever I reached this port again, to come and thank you for your love and kindness; — for," he added in a faltering voice, "to you, under God, do I owe all that I now am and all that I hope for hereafter. Had you been unsympathizing or discouraged, who knows where I might now have been?"

At the same time, and in the same school, was a girl, quick and bright of intellect, and attractive in personal appearance, but wild, careless, and irreverent in disposition, and devoted chiefly to dress, fashion, and every passing amusement. Caring, as she did, little for application in any pursuit, and disregarding home instructions, her teacher sought in vain to impress her with the importance of religious truths and duties, or with the solemn realities of a life to come.

Month after month she attended the school, and often her teacher was on the point of giving up what seemed a hopeless task, so little apparent influence did she exert over her. At length she removed to another city. Years passed on. Those who once were pupils had taken the places of teachers in the school, and still its usefulness was sustained. Nothing had been heard of Caroline B——, until, one Sabbath morning, a letter was handed to her old teacher, directed in a well-known hand. After giving an account of her new and pleasant home in the far West, and of the little family gathered around her, in touching terms she referred to the old schoolroom at ——, and of the many associations gathered around that spot. "Often and often have I thought of your kindness and of your instructions, and thanked God that you wearied not in what must have seemed such fruitless labors. I know I ridiculed and spurned them. But when laid for months on the bed of sickness, unable even to read, your gentle voice and those Sabbath lessons came back to me as freshly and as vividly as but yesterday. Your pleading and earnest words echoed and re-echoed through my soul, and when life and health slowly returned, I arose from my bed another and a different being. Life has become transfigured to me. The future is no longer a dream, nor eternity and retribution mere names. Gladly would

I pour forth my heart-felt thanks to you, but words are inadequate. In another world, next to the Saviour shall I thank you for your love to me, when I rendered no return."

Do not such incidents as these — and easily could they be multiplied — speak in earnest tones to every teacher of the duty of long-suffering patience, and a steady, hearty perseverance in the work? Shall we be so quick and ready to see the faults and be discouraged by the heedlessness of the little child, or the ardent, impetuous youth, when standing in such daily need ourselves of the Divine forbearance and forgiveness? Where should we be, were the Master as ready to mark our follies and sins, as we are to complain of those who often hear no words of religious instruction, save from our lips?

Let the teacher be diligent, faithful, and true, but *never* let him be discouraged in witnessing no immediate results of his labors. "First the blade, then the ear, after that the full corn in the ear."

Let him faithfully give line upon line, precept upon precept, never wearying of repeating the same explanations, patiently meeting the various wants of his pupils, and in trusting faith breaking to them the bread of life. Let him never give way to any feelings of impatience or irritability, or evince, by a careless, hurried manner, that he is weary of his work; but let him ever remember Him who is long-suffering and kind, even to the unthankful and the evil, and never feel discouraged, so long as he is conscious of having spoken and acted with the sincere purpose of following his divine Master.

" Speak gently to the erring ones,
They must have toiled in vain;
Perchance unkindness made them so;
O, win them back again!

" Speak gently, — 't is a little thing
Dropped in the heart's deep well;
The good, the joy, that it may bring
Eternity shall tell."

Patience and perseverance, learned from a holy communion with the Saviour's life and spirit, inwrought into the secret recesses of the soul, what qualifications more essential to the religious teacher! Patience towards others, patience with one's own heart, sustained by the steadfast, onward endeavor, and the quiet waiting upon God; a fixed and definite aim, upheld by a strong, resolute, and determined perseverance to go right onward, though no visible, immediate results are realized, — such a spirit does every teacher need.

To every one truly and heartily engaged in the work is it said, with a deep and abiding emphasis, "Be not *weary* in well-doing"; for the promise is sure and for ever, "In due season ye shall reap, if ye faint not."

CHAPTER VI.

QUALIFICATIONS OF THE TEACHER. — CHRISTIAN FAITH AND HOPEFULNESS.

"O help us, through the prayer of faith,
More firmly to believe;
For still the more the servant hath,
The more shall he receive."

"If ye have faith as a grain of mustard-seed," said our Saviour to his disciples, as, awe-struck and astonished, they witnessed the display of his miraculous power, "ye shall say unto this mountain, Remove hence to yonder place, and it shall remove; and nothing shall be impossible to you." In another place, as if to unfold to them yet more fully the profound and seemingly hidden mystery of his words, he adds, "What things soever ye desire when ye pray, believe that ye receive them, and ye shall have them."

Are not these words equally applicable to the Christian teacher of the present day as to those first disciples? However widely different in its peculiar circumstances and mere outward environments, is there not as deep a need *now* in the Church of Christ of this true, abiding faith, as in those earlier times, when trial and persecution were the certain results of a frank and honest avowal of the divine claims of the Redeemer?

Is not this faith greatly wanting among us? Have we not, to a great degree, lost a simple and practical trust in the power and efficacy of prayer, the one great means of sustaining a true and living faith? Believing, it may be, intellectually, in the promise of divine help and guidance, is there not among many a half-acknowledged feeling that prayer is only an act of self-excitation, a requisite form of the acknowledgment of the divine goodness and support, but bringing to the soul no peculiar benefits, no special blessing from the fount of divine truth and love? Is there not a too prevalent feeling of the necessary reliance upon God as the author of eternal law and order, as a Being unchangeable in his government, and for ever fixed in his wise and inscrutable decrees, without that reverential fear, that personal confidence, that holy trust, that sees in all a Father's hand, that believes in his direct, immediate communion with every soul, listening to the faintest prayer of the sincere and child-like spirit, and adapting every blessing, every trial, every event to the ultimate good of the individual soul, — yearning over it with a Father's tenderness, and satisfying its faintest desires from his own overflowing fulness and love?

The sublimest of the prophets, in the midst of his warnings and entreaties to the chosen people of Jehovah, speaks of the Holy One as "being afflicted in all the afflictions of his people." And will not such a view of the divine character, so tender, so compassionate, so congenial to the individual consciousness, alone prompt the sincere and heart-felt prayer, the earnest supplication for a faith like that which He revealed who ever dwelt in the bosom of the Father?

Is not such a faith, faint it may be at first, and often doubting and hesitating, but growing with the soul's growth, and daily increasing with its strength, is not such a faith an essential qualification for the teacher of religious truth?

Were we asked, indeed, to point out the quality which, more than any other, is needed to render one an effective and successful teacher of the young, we should reply at once and emphatically, Faith, — not a mere belief in the Gospel as a divine revelation, but a heart conscious of its power, and firmly relying on the Saviour's word of promise, "Whatsoever ye shall ask, believing, ye shall receive."

However humble, however diffident of his own strength, however young and inexperienced, if this principle dwell in his soul, the teacher will not hesitate to go right onward in duty, to meet the claims of others, however weighty, to speak the direct words of truth, or to make the urgent personal appeal, however difficult it may sometimes seem; for he will feel that not in his own strength does he stand, and that he is but the minister of One whose word of eternal truth remains sure and for ever: "My strength shall be made perfect in thy weakness."

To every such teacher we would say, first of all, cherish a just and true faith in *those whom* you teach. Going from week to week to your little class, accustomed to the same routine, meeting the same familiar faces, often repulsed by the cold word, the indifferent spirit, or the careless manner, witnessing no immediate fruits of your labors, called on again and again to repeat the same simple explanations, and often seeking, apparently in vain, to fix the wandering attention, you need to cherish a deep, abiding, and realizing sense of the unspeakable worth and value of every soul; to realize that you are speaking, not to the mere transient beings of a summer's day, but to immortal spirits, — spirits that cannot die; spirits which the Eternal Father created and loves, and for which Christ lived and died; souls, one moment of whose conscious existence infolds greater mysteries than the most profound philosophy can disclose; capable of rising upwards to heights of glory, purity, and holiness, now faintly imagined even in its highest and boldest aspirations, or of sinking into that spiritual darkness and death which He, who well knew the strength and the weakness, the good and the evil, in each human soul, so fearfully and so solemnly imaged as the region of outer darkness, "where the worm dieth not and the fire is not quenched."

Study your own soul. Look searchingly and carefully within. Learn its powers and capacities of progress and advancement, its powers of thought and aspiration and growing holiness, its capacities of love and sympathy and self-sacrifice, and of heavenly faith and communion; read within, in every line and fibre of your intellectual and moral being, the hand of the Almighty Creator, for ever pointing out your true relationship to him, in a holy, child-like dependence, and teaching you to turn away from all self-reliance and self-worship to Him who discerneth the very thoughts afar off, without whose intimate, constant presence in the soul not even thought could perform its simplest functions or the spirit wing one earnest aspiration upward. Learn, from close self-examination, from a true and just self-knowledge, springing from the depths of lowly prayer, and holy communion, and a sense of inward want and deficiency; learn, too, the reality of the soul's sinfulness, of its alienation from God, of the perversion of its noble powers, and the waste of its glorious inheritance; learn that in itself it is weak and helpless and sinful, and that only through the divine renewal can it be brought into its true relationship with the Unseen, — that only through its second and true birth into the spiritual life can it know aught of the blessedness of reconciliation and pardon, and of oneness with God through Christ.

Look earnestly and truly within; and as the great facts of your moral being become distinctly imaged to your soul, as they become eternal realities to you, far more than the mere transient events and fading glitter of the outward world, as you contemplate the soul's immortal destiny, and the momentous results that flow from its present solemn choice between the great opposing forces that now divide the moral universe, you will feel more and more that in every human spirit there are infolded powers and capacities, heights and depths of being, far transcending in grandeur and solemn interest a whole universe of material worlds. As this consciousness becomes indelibly impressed on your soul, you will meet your pupils from week to week, no longer in mere outward form, but with the abiding conviction that you are holding communion with immortal souls; with an assured faith that in every child, however ignorant, however uninteresting to the common observer, however careless or indifferent, there dwells a living spirit, — a spirit that shall still exist when suns and worlds and countless systems shall have passed from being.

Could every teacher come to his class from Sabbath to Sabbath, "penetrated with a living conviction of the grandeur, the infinitude, the preciousness of the soul of every pupil; could he escape from the benumbing influences of habit, and the constant tendency of details to fritter away reverence and tame wonder down; could he keep his realizing perception of what a soul is as vivid as if the revelation of it were made each instant afresh to his own mind, — it is safe to say, not merely that harvests, richer than his boldest hope dared dream of, would crown his toil, — an unprecedented intensity touching his Christ-like lips with inspiration, and clothing every word with wings of fire, — but also that a zeal for the task would seize on his own heart, sending him to it with an impulse that he could not keep back, and would make his every message like a chapter from the gospel of life."

Have faith, we repeat, in *those whom* you teach. Cherish a trusting confidence in the child. Believe that your fervent prayers of intercession in his behalf will assuredly be answered, though it may be in a way and at a time now unknown to you. Have faith, that, if under God you can awaken or strengthen in that young soul a desire and a longing for its heavenly inheritance, One, to whom that spirit's life is infinitely precious, will ever work with and in him both to will and to do, of his good pleasure.

Have faith in what you teach; for it is the eternal truth of God;— not mere facts of human wisdom, not the traditions of human authority, not the perplexing theories of philosophers, not the vain speculations of the theorist, or the merely fanciful dreams of the spiritualist, are you called on to weigh, discuss, and teach; but those simple, solemn, and sublime truths, which constitute the very essence and attributes of the Eternal, which God has written in part on the soul itself, and which he has yet more clearly revealed through the life and mission of his Son.

Never feel that it is *your* truth that you are imparting, for such teaching may well prove vain. Speak in the Master's name and spirit, with faith that his teachings received into the soul can remove even mountains of sin and evil. Believe in his divine power. Cherish the full assurance that He who at a single touch could send the thrill of life through the palsied limb, and whose word alone poured light upon eyes long quenched in gloom and darkness, can equally awaken the soul from its lethargic slumber of indifference and sin, and shed celestial light over its darkened being.

Measure not the divine power by your own weakness and helplessness; distrust not the divine resources. Think not, that, because you witness no present fruits, the seed of truth contains no germ of a living life.

> "God moves in a mysterious way
> His wonders to perform";

and often may verdure and bloom and gladness spring forth in souls which to human sight seemed all waste, barren, and unfruitful.

Rest your confidence firmly and exclusively on the word of God, and accept his promises as addressed to you personally. By faith go forth and labor, and through faith endure, as seeing Him who is invisible; relying not on what you can accomplish or perform, but only on what God has promised to do in and through you.

So cherish a true and just, though humble, faith in your *power* to teach. There is such a thing as a vain self-distrust, and a false humility, based, not on a Christ-like lowliness of spirit, but on a lack of confidence in God, and a questioning of the divine omnipotence. It hesitates to speak and act, not so much from conscious weakness and ignorance as from an unwillingness to trust in the divine promise, to give itself wholly up to the guidance of the Spirit, and to become simply the conscious and willing medium of the divine blessing to other souls. It seeks to work in its own way, to lay out its own plans, to accomplish something great and noble as of itself, — instead of laying its firm hold on the Divine hand let down for its guidance and support. Such self-distrust, such easy discouragement, has never learned the lesson of a true self-renunciation; for too often it arises from an undue self-appreciation, which asks not in lowly prayer only to be, in *God's* own way, a ministering servant unto others.

Let the teacher cherish an earnest desire to carry the message of Christ's truth to other souls, relying solely on his promise of help and blessing; let him cherish a living faith *in those whom* he teaches, in the eternal reality of *what* he teaches, and he will seldom doubt his *power* to teach. He will no longer be anxiously questioning what others may think of him, or whether his success be greater or less; but the truth realized in his own secret consciousness, the love of Christ filling his soul, will compel him to the work. It will be harder for him to refrain from entering the field, or to quit the service, than to toil earnestly, laboriously, and truly. He knows that his Master is there, and under his standard would he endure the same toils and difficulties, humbly trusting likewise to share with him the same eternal joy and blessedness.

Have faith, then, in your *power* to teach; for, as it was given to the early disciples, in the hour of danger and of trial, what they ought to speak, even so shall your soul, resting wholly upon God, be filled with the Spirit, and your tongue shall be kindled as with the fire of inspiration, and your lips shall glow with the burning utterance of truth.

Look upward ever. Catch your inspiration from the Saviour's own lips. Grasp the hand even now stretched forth to guide and lead you. Accept the proffered help and the tender sympathy. Be of good courage; rise, for it is no human voice, but the Master that calleth thee, that bids thee cast aside the fear and the doubt and the hesitancy, and to enter joyfully and courageously into his service. He bids thee gird on the armor and put on the breast-plate of faith and love, and, "strong in utter weakness," to be his now and for ever.

How has this earnest, conscious, trusting faith shed the brightest radiance over the darkest passages of human life, and enriched its barren and desolate wastes with a heavenly beauty and a divine glory! Its light has pierced the captive's cell, and often poured its holiest beams amid the gloom and darkness of the dungeon; it has cheered the wanderer on his solitary path, and strengthened the lonely missionary to deeds of noble self-sacrifice and cheerful self-renunciation; it has filled the home of the poor with riches far surpassing the splendor and the glory of Solomon, — and by its side, in the rich man's home, the countless treasures of wealth and luxury look dim and pale; it lights the brow of childhood with a gentler beauty, and places the crown of patient endurance on the head of saintly womanhood; it sheds its own holy and blessed radiance around the bed of sickness and of suffering, and encircles the brow of the dying with a celestial glory; and over the silence of the grave it places the unfading bow of celestial promise, encircling both worlds in its beautiful embrace, and whispering in gentle accents those inspiring words, "He is not here, he is risen."

How many and noble have been the instances in which this living faith has girded even the fearful and timid soul to deeds of noble heroism and sublime sacrifice, and enabled the spirit to press patiently and faithfully onward in daily duty, even though surrounded by darkness, trial, and discouragement! How is the cold hesitancy of the mere worldling, and the timid faith of the half-believer, rebuked by these examples of a holy and sublime trust, — the world's richest and noblest inheritance!

When we read of the noble "Apostle to the Indians," who so richly merited this significant title, devoting, in entire faith, the powers of a strong intellect and the vigorous years of a faithful and active life to the laborious task of translating the Scriptures into an unwritten and savage tongue, that he might better convey the Gospel of divine truth to the unlettered and ignorant tribes among whom he so zealously labored; when we remember the devoted Cheverus, inflamed with an equal zeal and faith, encountering hardship and severe privations amid the primeval forests of Maine, surrounded by uncivilized Indians, or lovingly and unostentatiously laboring among scenes of poverty, distress, and pestilence in the crowded streets of the metropolis of New England, or when in the Archbishop's palace, surrounded by luxury, wealth, and refinement, the great and the noble deemed it an honor to claim him as their guest whom no elevation, no worldly distinction or power, could render less simple and loving or less devoted to his Master's work; when we recall the native enthusiasm of Loyola, first baptized and consecrated by a religious faith and hope on the couch of sickness and suffering, which, to human sight, seemed destined to destroy his fondest hopes and anticipations, but by the divine blessing became to him as the entrance to a new and spiritual life, — his soul being so pervaded and filled with ardent zeal and an aspiring faith, that henceforth no effort was too laborious, no sacrifice too great, no suffering too severe, for him to encounter in the service of his Lord; when we remember Luther's bold promulgation of the Apostolic doctrine of justification by faith alone, by which he turned the world upside down, breaking the chains of a self-righteous morality and a self-sufficient piety; when we remember Wilberforce, with a Christ-like faith and love toiling for years amid opposition, obloquy, and scorn in the great cause of human brotherhood and freedom; when we go back in thought to those earlier days of the Church, when the acknowledgment of a Christian faith was the seal of persecution and death, and remember those whose only homes were among the catacombs of the imperial city or in wild and desert places, their only refuge from the bitter tyranny of oppression; when we number the long array of noble witnesses to Christ; of martyrs, ambitious only to suffer for their Master; of holy men in every age, who have loved truth more than worldly honor and distinction; of reformers, who have boldly braved sceptical taunts and cold sneers, and with unflinching purpose pressed boldly on in their earnest endeavors for the attainment of a higher truth and right; of missionaries, true to their calling in the midst of discouragement and weakness, counting it all joy if they might plant the single seed of truth, perchance the germ of future harvests alone; when such men as Schwartz and Martyn, Boardman, Judson, and Hall, Neff, and Oberlin, rise before us in their self-sacrificing devotedness and holy trust; when we recall the names of those less conspicuous to the world's eye, but none the less true and devoted in a different sphere, — the noble Lady Huntington, the practical Hannah Moore, the zealous Catharine

Adorna, the gentle Elizabeth Carter, the self-sacrificing Mrs. Fry, the true and faithful Mary Ware, — we feel that there is a *reality* in the Christian faith, a power to lift the soul above all selfish considerations, to transform it into the Saviour's image, and to make it one with God. We can no longer question or coldly doubt its divine and inherent force, for its quickening pulse beats through our veins, and its sympathetic thrill nerves our weak and often faint endeavors, as we read of that glorious crowd of witnesses, who, having maintained a good confession, have entered into the joy of their Lord.

Not alone to those distinguished by peculiar trials or sufferings, or occupying conspicuous stations in life, would we look. We would also remember those whose path has been among the sheltered scenes of life, in homes of holy love; whose daily toil has been sanctified by the spirit of prayer; whose self-sacrificing devotedness to others has been surpassed by none for whom the world claims the crown of an immortal saintship; who have patiently watched by the couch of lingering disease and chronic infirmity, and calmly stood by the dying-bed of those most dear, commending the parting soul, in the spirit of an entire submission and a holy trust, to the Father of all. We would remember those who, in the Saviour's spirit, have gathered the wandering and outcast, the children of ignorance and sin, and in simple reliance on the divine word of promise, have gone from house to house, breaking to them the bread of life; those who have been unwearied amid the cares and perplexities of daily life, and whose lamp of love has ever been kept trimmed and burning; who through faith in God have met discouragement and disappointment, and transformed every trial into a means of heavenly growth and progress.

As this nearer cloud of witnesses gathers around us, with their words of holy love, as we recognize the familiar countenances of those who have cheered us on life's pilgrimage, or the secret and hallowed influence of whose characters has quickened in our souls a nobler aspiration and a holier trust, we feel and believe more deeply the reality of that spirit of faith through which they conquered, and by which we also may attain. It is no longer a mere word, but a working force and an active power, felt in the secret depths of the soul, bringing it into a nearer communion with the Saviour's spirit, and into a holier harmony with God.

When, in the hour of secret thought and heavenly communion, the Christian teacher remembers those committed to his charge, and bears them in his heart in his earnest prayer of intercession, let him ever pray in this spirit of confiding faith, looking not for immediate success or an earthly recompense of reward, but believing that every seed of holy and right endeavor, however humble, will bear its true and ripened fruit,

"In those everlasting gardens,
Where angels walk, and seraphs are the wardens;
Where every flower brought safe through death's dark portal
Becomes immortal."

CHAPTER VII.

QUALIFICATIONS OF THE TEACHER. — MENTAL ENDOWMENTS AND SPECIAL PREPARATION.

"To serve the present age,
My calling to fulfil,
O, may it *all* my powers engage
To do my Master's will!"

HAVING spoken of some of the spiritual traits of character, and the heart qualifications, to be faithfully sought and cultivated by every true teacher, we would now pass to considerations of a more intellectual nature, and to those mental qualities essential to render one a successful and effective teacher of the young.

Going into almost any of our Sunday schools, and carefully watching the working of the whole system as it now exists, the observer is at once impressed with the fact that there are not apparent that progress, order, unity, and system, which so strikingly characterize the best conducted of our public schools. Children of all ages and capacities are admitted, and often classed with little reference to their various degrees of mental and moral advancement; they remain with the same teacher for a longer or shorter time, too often according to the mere caprice of the child or the wishes or capacity of the teacher; they are then transferred to another class; the manual already used for many months is perhaps recommenced; often the teacher or superintendent makes no thorough examination of the pupil, to ascertain the true amount of his knowledge, and months and even years are passed without any definite, real progress being made. Sabbath after Sabbath he attends, but finds that no more knowledge is imparted to him than he has already gained by a cursory study of his prescribed lesson at home. He has learned the first lessons of religious truth, committed the simple hymns of childhood, studied the Gospels with the aid of some manual or commentary, and then, finding that no new field of thought and inquiry is open to him, he naturally becomes indifferent to his lessons; the school hour offers no excitement, no *stimulus*, to his mental powers, and an irregular attendance or a divided attention soon manifests his loss of interest.

Is such a result the fault of the child or the youth alone, as the teacher is too apt to imagine? As he attends the day-school, he is conscious from week to week of progress, — that most powerful stimulus to every aspiring, active mind, and he is sure of finding in his teacher one capable of leading him on in his studies, and directing his inquiries; and if faithful to himself, he knows that, at the close of the year, he will stand on a higher plane than at its commencement. His powers are taxed, his capacities developed, his reason and judgment strengthened by use, his imagination roused, and his curiosity excited. When he turns to the Sabbath school, he feels a want of impetus, a want of systematic progress, of growing intellectual attainment. We have known a child kept for two or three years studying the same little catechism or manual, because the whole was not faithfully committed to memory, to be recited *verbatim*, until its very sight awakened a feeling of disgust. Now, thorough teaching we would advocate as strongly and as urgently as any one, but we are very sure that thoroughness is not to be attained in this mechanical, dispiriting way. We remember attending once the examination of a high school, in company with a friend whose Sabbath scholars were pupils of the institution; and recollect the astonishment she expressed in finding them so far advanced in their studies, capable of performing difficult problems in mathematics, and of passing a good examination in natural philosophy, grammar, French, &c. It was a speaking and emphatic rebuke for her own neglect in ascertaining the true capacities of her pupils, and in preparing herself to meet their higher and more spiritual wants.

Is not such the case in a greater or less degree in all our schools? Must there not be a growth in some degree commensurate with the progress made in our secular schools, if we would have the instructions of the Sabbath vital and life-giving? Must we not have a more definite system of instruction, a more regular, progressive, thorough course of study pursued, commencing with the child's earliest years, and continuing until he leaves the school, or takes, himself, the place of a teacher?

Not that we would advocate a slavish conformity to a prescribed rule, or feel that every child needed or was capable of pursuing the same course of study. This would be utterly impossible in the present state of our schools, where some children attend but few months, others a year, and others still many years. If the instructions were more definitely systematized, and the schools better classified, we believe that much might be done towards the attainment of this end.

As the first essential step towards such a desirable attainment, as the first requisite to meet this imperative need of our schools as they now exist, we would speak of the necessity of teachers being truly *qualified* for their work.

Many seem to feel, that, intellectually speaking, a general knowledge of the facts of Gospel history is all that is needed to enable them to become teachers of the young; that, .f they can hear the simple lessons recited, or give some general explanations gleaned hastily from a popular commentary, it is all that is essential.

Here lies a most fatal error; for how are religious truths to be rendered attractive and interesting, without thorough preparation on the teacher's part, any more than the truths of science or the formulas of mathematics? A child is far less easily satisfied than an adult with half-explanations and a mere superficial knowledge, and he soon discovers whether he can rely upon his teacher for real assistance.

Take even the best conducted of our schools, and how few of the teachers could pass any good examination in the very fundamentals of Christian truth, in the evidences of religion, the proofs of the genuineness of the Gospels, and their his tory and transmission! How few, too, possess any distinct idea of the harmony of the Gospel narratives, of the occasions on which the Epistles were written, and the causes which immediately dictated them; while with many more the Old Testament, with its rich stores of biography, history, poetry, and prophecy, is regarded with utter indifference; and the origin and history of the Jewish faith in its peculiar relation to Christianity is considered as of little moment! How little definite information does there exist, too, of the relation of Christianity to the general history of the world, of its influence upon art, civilization, and language!

Why should teachers, thus unprepared by a proper course of study for their work, be employed in our Sabbath schools any more than in our common schools? Why should they not be required to pass an examination in certain studies before assuming such a responsibility? Would it not be more for the interests of our schools in general to have fewer teachers, and these *thoroughly* fitted for their work, than to have so much vague, indefinite teaching as is now often given? Much as we approve of the division of our schools into small classes, where alone the teacher can become intimately acquainted with the peculiar dispositions, wants, and temptations of each pupil, and thus adapt his instruction accordingly, we have sometimes thought that it would be better to have larger divisions, under the care of competent instructors, than to have so many uneducated teachers employed.

In speaking of the requisite qualifications of the teacher, we would not be unmindful of those who are in *heart* devoted to the work, but who possess little leisure or opportunity to pursue a course of intellectual study, or an examination into the higher branches of Christian truth.

Minds of every class are needed among us, provided they are only *awake*, *earnest*, and *faithful*.

To one unable to learn from books to any wide extent, the great and constantly varying lessons of daily life are ever opened, and from these he may draw ceaseless instruction.

An active, inquiring mind is the first intellectual requisite, — a mind constantly *growing*, constantly gaining new accessions of strength and power, through the trials and joys, the duties and the discipline, of each passing day. Every little circumstance, every passing incident, every varied phenomenon of the outward world, may be made conducive to the greater interest of one's teachings; he will treasure them up as means of illustrating the highest spiritual truths, of first awakening the curiosity or fixing the wandering attention.

For instance; one Sabbath morning, a class of little girls had for their appointed lesson a portion of the Sermon on the Mount. The words were familiar to them, and half a dozen verses were correctly repeated. But their thoughts were evidently anywhere but on the lesson. Instead of directly reproving them, however, or in set terms asking their attention, their teacher showed them a small twig of the chestnut-tree, which she had carefully broken off the day before, and began by explaining to them the wonderful manner in which the germ of the new green leaves were all enfolded in the bud, so carefully preserved amid the snows and cold of winter, how the sap circulated through each minute fibre, and the warm spring sunshine and the gentle rains pierced the outer casement, until the first delicate green of the leaf appeared, to be so soon succeeded by the darker hue and the denser shades of the summer foliage. Her object was gained, — an interest was excited; and turning again to the simple words, "Consider the lilies of the field," a lesson upon the constant goodness and love of God was imparted, which no formal repetition of truths would ever have impressed.

So should it ever be with the teacher. He should never feel that his work for the week is finished, when he has studied the appointed lesson or when the school hour is over. His preparation is *never* completed, for it is co-extensive with his moral and intellectual advantages, and with the whole discipline of life. The best and most effective preachers are those who the most faithfully garner up the lessons of each passing day and make them conducive to the highest spiritual ends; and so is it with the Sunday-school teacher, — for he also is a pastor, he also has a flock committed to his keeping, and equally momentous and solemn, though not equally extensive, are his responsibilities.

Such a *daily* preparation every teacher is bound to make, however limited his sphere or however narrow his means of intellectual culture; and

where such preparation is united with the spiritual qualifications already considered, we shall always find effective, useful, and faithful teachers, though they may not be qualified to carry on their pupils in the study of the highest branches of religious truth.

To the many in our schools who have enjoyed the advantages and opportunities of a more liberal culture we would say emphatically, that the standard of intellectual fitness for their work is altogether too low, and one great cause of the want of a higher and truer success.

As the next requisite for a good teacher, we would place the possession of definite, clear, and accurate ideas upon the subjects taught. It is surprising to find how many undertake to impart a knowledge of the most momentous of all themes, to speak upon subjects the highest and most sublime that can ever occupy the human mind, whose own views are crude, unsettled, and indefinite.

New truths will, of course, be constantly unfolding to the inquiring mind, but there must be some firm, definite substratum of faith, on which to found any real progress; and this can only be gained by patient thought, careful investigation, and a diligent study of the Word of Truth. Every teacher should have definite ideas of the great truths of Christian doctrine,— of the being and attributes of God, of the nature and offices

of Christ, of the soul's need of redemption, of salvation through a crucified Saviour, of retribution and eternity. These views should be distinctly imaged to his own soul, or he will surely fail in imparting them distinctly and clearly to others. Can they be obtained simply through a mechanical acceptance of the truth? Is not the teacher thus wronging both his own soul and those of his pupils? Dogmatic teaching we would be far from advocating, neither would we have the sacred hours of the Sabbath devoted to the mere critical discussion of disputed doctrines. But if the teacher would faithfully consider the wants of his pupils, and distinctly meet the questions that arise, incidentally at least, in almost every lesson, he must have his own settled and definite views of truth. He must constantly seek for such; must ever inquire more and more earnestly into the hidden secrets of divine wisdom; must make it his fixed aim to attain to clear convictions on these most important themes.

Nothing is more fatal to success than a want of clearness in the teacher's own mind; for where a subject is thoroughly comprehended, there is seldom a lack of definite expression. Such definiteness is needed, not only in relation to the higher themes of truth, but also in connection with every subject embraced within the wide range of Christian teaching. Take the simplest lesson, and let it be repeated in a merely mechanical manner, and then observe how different will be the interest excited, if the teacher be able to illustrate its varied incidents and truths by a vivid description of the places mentioned, by an accurate account of the manners and customs prevalent at the time, by alluding to contemporary events, and showing the influence of Christianity in moulding the habits and modes of life of various nations. Then let him pass on to the clear enforcement of the direct truths springing from the subject, and the lesson becomes simply the nucleus for imparting a large amount of useful knowledge and high spiritual truth.

The practical teacher needs, also, to cultivate the habit of close and accurate observation, in order to store his mind with ready illustrations, and to enable him the more easily and truly to read the characters of those committed to his care. A great part of the mistakes and failures in our schools arise from the true nature and character of the pupil being misunderstood; and this power or capacity of comprehending another mind can be gained only by a faithful study of one's own spirit, and by a true and heartfelt sympathy with others, united with a quick perception of, and a close attention to, all those nameless trifling incidents that so often more clearly reveal the true character than any striking act or great deed.

A teacher had in her class a pupil very uninteresting in manners and appearance, seemingly cold and indifferent, and who could rarely be induced to answer even a single question before others. The teacher observed her attentively, but could gain little insight into her real character. One Sabbath, she watched the changing expression of her countenance, and the animation that lighted up her face, as she read the sublime words of one of the old Hebrew prophets. A key to her hitherto concealed feelings was at once given. Beneath that cold exterior, and diffident, almost repulsive manner, there was a hidden enthusiasm, a deep love of the poetical, and an appreciation of the beautiful, that few understood. The teacher at once addressed herself to this trait of character, and the pupil soon felt that she was no longer apart from others,—that one, at least, understood and sympathized with her. The ice was broken; confidence took the place of a cold reserve, and there is now no more interesting and attentive pupil in the class than Ellen B——.

This same habit of observation should also be cultivated with regard to all the wonderful phenomena of the outward universe; for what more conducive to the purity and elevation of the soul than an habitual communion with God through his works; and what more fruitful source of instruction and illustration to the teacher is there than this? A love of what is beautiful and wonderful in the creation is natural to the child. To his opening mind everything around him is full of mystery, and how easy to lead those questioning thoughts up to the great Author and Giver of all good!

The glad sunshine and the darkened cloud, the gentle summer shower and the fierce winter's storm, the delicate spring flower and the gorgeous autumn foliage, the tiny pebble on the seashore and the variegated moss that fringes the mountain-pine, the murmuring stream and the thundering cataract, the wild music of the ocean's ceaseless roar, and the solemn cadence of the vast and mighty forests, — all are full of lessons of the highest wisdom, power, and goodness; all are unfailing sources through which to teach the child of that great and holy Being, upon whose goodness he constantly and ceaselessly depends. Still greater will be the interest excited, if to the mere observation and love of the beautiful in nature the teacher adds some definite knowledge of the laws of science and of art, and is able to illustrate how, in the most common phenomena of daily life, the same eternal law and order are visible, — regulating the falling of the stone from the green hillside and guiding the most distant planet in its vast and solemn orbit, painting the dew-drop on the summer's morn and arching the heavens with the bow of eternal promise, touching the autumn foliage with its gorgeous tints, and covering the mighty waters as with a breastplate. Never let him speak of these laws, or of the regular and beautiful order of nature, as mere cold abstractions. Let him teach the child of the Father's hand, as the one sole mover and upholder of all, the one first and only cause, dwelling in and through all things, whose agency is ceaselessly present in each ray of light, each springing blade of grass, each sparkling dew-drop, and each changing leaf; whose love is manifest in the choral song of birds and the humming of insects, and the gladness of all animated creation; in the freshness and brightness of the early morn, and the solemn stillness and hushed silence of the night season; in the fragrance and beauty of the simplest flower, and the ever-varying and wonderful beauty of the passing clouds, arching the heavens as with a divine glory and radiance.

Never let him teach of the powers of nature as something distinct and separate from God,— as if nature were a perfect machine, once set in motion and eternally reproducing her own works, — as if the Eternal dwelt afar off, and took no immediate care or concern of his infinite creation; but let him teach of the Omnipresent Father, whose power is as directly manifest in the summer breeze and the gently waving foliage as in the mighty whirlwind and fierce winter's storm; who blends each ray of glad and cheerful light with the same eternal wisdom and power that guide Arcturus and Orion in their courses, whose watchfulness is as direct and constant over the most transient insect of a summer's day as over the movement of mighty suns and systems.

Let the thought of God's constant presence be thus brought very near to the soul; let it be inwrought into the child's daily life and conscious existence; let it be so inseparably united with all his varied experience, that nothing shall ever shake its assured reality or lead him to doubt the almighty power, the eternal wisdom, and the unchangeable goodness of Him upon whom he daily and hourly depends, — whose thoughts are not as our thoughts, and whose ways are often inscrutable and past finding out; but who, in the blessed revelation of his Son, has made himself known as the Father of all, the God of perfect love and holiness, ever abiding with the soul that turns to Him with a child-like confidence and a reverential trust.

The teacher needs especially a thorough and growing knowledge of the Scriptures. He should never rest satisfied with a merely general, superficial acquaintance with their contents, or feel that he has ever fathomed their full meaning, for the study of a lifetime could not exhaust their rich treasures of spiritual instruction. He should feel it to be his duty, as well as his privilege, to be constantly gaining new light from every available source, to be seeking new and more enlarged views of truth and duty, and to enter more and more into the comprehension of their sublime and momentous revelations. He needs not merely a knowledge of the facts of the Gospels, but a definite idea of the harmony of the different narratives, of the convincing proofs of their genuineness and authenticity, and of the preservation of their contents from the earliest time, amid the ignorance and superstition of the Dark Ages, the bitter strife and persecution of rival sects, and the domineering spirit of mere partisanship and personal ambition. He needs also to study carefully the Epistles, with their rich treasures of thought and spiritual experience, and to become familiar with the writings of those who were the personal disciples and immediate followers of Christ, who were solemnly commissioned and peculiarly endowed by him to preach the Gospel, and to spread abroad the truth which he lived, suffered, and died to establish in the world. The writings of Paul, particularly, studied carefully and thoughtfully, will no longer be regarded as obscure and unedifying, as is so often the case even with intelligent persons. To many his Epistles have been, and will ever remain, as sealed books; but not necessarily so. Let them only be approached in the wide and catholic spirit in which they were written, with some adequate conception of their general design, scope, and purpose; let them be read carefully and diligently, without reference to sect or creed or party; let their spirit of fervent love, of living earnestness, of deep spirituality and kindling faith, be in some measure comprehended and felt, and they cannot be read or studied without advantage and interest. New depths of thought, new forms of beauty, new conceptions of truth, will constantly reveal themselves to the diligent seeker, and Paul will no longer seem as a mere abstract conception, but as a living, personal, sympathizing friend, pre-eminently worthy of being a chosen servant of Christ, the Apostle to the Gentiles, and the preacher of Christianity to the whole world, in all ages and in all climes.

The Old Testament, with its rich stores of life and of wisdom, its history and biography, its poetry and prophecy, is regarded by many at the present time with growing or utter indifference, and often wholly excluded from the religious instruction of the young. But what a wide field of study and research is here open to the faithful teacher! Extending back to that earliest and unknown period of time when, in the midst of chaotic darkness the sublime mandate was first uttered, "Let there be light," and thence onward, through succeeding centuries, and the varied history of the human race, when the darkness of ignorance and sin was from time to time illuminated by the light of prophecy, and the examples of holy and faithful men, who placed a firm, implicit reliance on the covenant word of promise; until, as the ages rolled on, the brightness of a more glorious day appeared, "shedding light on the waning star of Jacob and the darkened fortunes of the house of David."

The teacher needs, especially, to have some distinct and definite understanding of the true authority of these separate books, so rich in instruction and interest; to be well versed in their ample stores of biography and historical wealth, and to be especially familiar with their sublime strains of prayer and of worship. "He should also be conversant with the leading facts of ecclesiastical history, the geography of the religious world, the distinctive marks of the chief Christian sects, and the lives and services of the representative men of different ages and sections of the Church." He needs, too, to have distinct and clearly defined views upon the authority of a divine revelation as established and confirmed by miracle.

At the present time, when there exists so much scepticism upon the very fundamentals of Christian truth, — when, by many, faith is merged in scientific knowledge, and all truth rejected that cannot be fully comprehended by human reason or measured and defined as by geometrical rule and line; when cold Rationalism is substituted for ardent piety, and a self-sufficient righteousness for faith in Christ, — when there exists, especially among those just entering upon early manhood, so much love of doubting, and that pride of reason which is constantly questioning the plainest truths of revelation, and imagines that it is exalting itself whenever it can seemingly falsify some long-accepted truth by the skilful use of its newly acquired logic, though it leaves nothing in its place but barren formulas and a cold scepticism, — the Christian teacher needs, with new care and with new zeal and earnestness, to re-examine the grounds of his belief, and to be sure that he is able to impart to others definite ideas and convincing proofs of the faith he teaches.

Let him not vainly endeavor to bound his instructions or his faith by the limitations of human knowledge, or be afraid sometimes to assert on the authority of Scripture what passes his own reason. "Every great spiritual doctrine terminates in mystery, by the very necessity of spirit. The essence of faith is a reverential confession of the limitations of sight." So should the teacher, ever seeking higher and wider views of truth, still bow in reverential awe and holy trust before the Infinite and the Unknown, and remember that the noblest and highest intellect can only exclaim, in deep humility, "How unsearchable are his judgments, and his ways past finding out!" "Now we see as through a glass, darkly; but *then* face to face!"

He should seek, by the faithful use of every opportunity he may enjoy, to develop and strengthen his mental powers, to add to his already acquired knowledge, and to enrich his mind from the treasures of literature, art, science, and poetry. His reason should be often employed upon such subjects as tax the powers of the mind, and require real thought and close application; his judgment should be strengthened by exercise and a keen observation of the passing events of daily life; his imagination cultivated and restrained, and his taste purified and educated,—all this, not merely for his own sake, but to render him better qualified to teach even the simplest truths to others. Even the more abstruse studies of mathematics, or the acquirement of foreign languages, or a familiar acquaintance with the higher walks of literature, will not be as useless wealth to their possessor; for a mind, rich, cultivated, and constantly progressing, will ever make its true momentum felt. How magical the charm that such a mind can throw over the most familiar and worn-out truths, by the power of illustration and analogy, by a full appreciation of the subject, and a good degree of enthusiasm in delineating it to others!

How much can such a teacher effect in forming the tastes and intellectual habits of his pupils, without any apparent direct effort to this end! He can stimulate them to greater diligence in their studies, point out to them instructive and useful courses of reading, interest them in the wonders of science, incite them to higher aims by references to the biographies of the great and good, quicken their observation of the boundless works of nature, and, through his own active and earnest spirit, insensibly lead them to loftier aims and nobler attainments.

A teacher thus qualified for his work will never bound his instructions by any given manual. He will, indeed, teach thoroughly and systematically, but having faithfully studied the given lesson, he will find it necessary rather to select from the abundance of his materials than to be casting about to discover what he can say, or how he may occupy the given hour. Like the faithful pastor, he will be constantly gathering up new stores of wisdom, and well feel that even his leisure hours are to be made subservient to his highest intellectual and moral progress.

Some may assert, that few have the opportunity to make this thorough preparation for their work, or are able thus to fit themselves to be teachers to the more advanced pupils. With many, is not the *aim*, the *desire*, rather than the ability or opportunity, wanting? Do we not often find among those who are the most busily occupied during the week those who have made the most self-improvement, and who are the most faithful in seeking to prepare themselves for their duties as teachers? Often those who have enjoyed the best advantages of education, and who possess the most leisure, make the least effective teachers; for it is the *spirit* and the *earnest desire* of improvement, rather than the amount gained, that constitute the true momentum of character. He who improved the two talents committed to his charge received the same commendation with the recipient of the five; it was the slothful, negligent servant who was rebuked and rejected.

Were this higher intellectual culture, this spirit of self-improvement, regarded as *essential* by the teachers of our schools, we should no longer complain of the prevalent want of progress. If we are to look to those, now pupils, who leave these schools from year to year, to be in their turn teachers of others, how imperative the need that they should be thoroughly instructed in all the branches of a true Christian faith!

"*What is to be done* to render our schools more efficient and useful?" is a question again and again asked. We reply at once, and emphatically, — next to the spiritual culture already considered, — *Educate teachers thoroughly for their work.* Begin by adopting some simple criterion, by requiring some definite qualifications in the teacher, ere he takes charge of a class, however young or ignorant. Enough has there been of mere hap-hazard teaching, enough of random, indefinite teaching. Would we see a thorough reform in our whole system, we must begin at the fountain-head. It must be *distinctly understood*, that no one can become a teacher in the Sabbath school, without due *preparation*, any more than a teacher in a public day-school.

Since we are now laboring under the disadvantages and errors resulting from this want of preparation, and of personal fitness for the office, we would suggest, as some remedy for the evil, that the teachers of our several schools be required to meet at stated times, to pursue regular courses of reading, study, and inquiry, under the direction of some competent teacher or superintendent, or of the pastor, if he have the leisure to devote to this end. Let every teacher who is not already well versed in the subject be required to attend such meetings, and to make himself thoroughly master of the lesson. Even one hour a week occupied thus systematically and thoroughly would do much toward the bringing in of a better state of things, especially if it were distinctly understood that none but those who are seeking to *fit themselves* for the work can be received as teachers.

For the attainment of such an end, every teacher is individually responsible. He should magnify his office. He should feel the solemn obligation that rests upon him to render his own work thorough and complete, knowing that nothing can be trifling or worthless that has an eternal influence over other souls; and that only as he improves his daily opportunities, only as he cultivates the talents committed to his keeping, will it be said, in the solemn day of account, "Well done, good and faithful servant; thou hast been faithful over a few things, I will make thee ruler over many things: enter thou into the joy of thy Lord."

CHAPTER VIII.

DUTIES OF THE TEACHER.

> " Soldiers of Christ, arise !
> And gird your armor on !
> Strong in the strength which God suppiies,
> Through his beloved Son."

THE disciple of Christ, as he undertakes the office of a Christian teacher, asks at once and earnestly, What are some of the peculiar duties now incumbent on me? What new responsibilities do I incur, as I enter on this field of labor? What direct preparation must I make for meeting my class from Sabbath to Sabbath, in order to render my instructions vital and effective?

The more general answers to these questions have already been given, in considering the spiritual and intellectual qualifications of the teacher; but there are yet minor details, too important to be wholly passed over, implied, indeed, in what has already been said, but which it may be well to consider in their more direct, imn ε-diate bearing.

First, it is the duty of the teacher to set apart some regular hour for the faithful study and preparation of the immediate lesson of the day. No matter how familiar he may be with its contents, how simple is the instruction to be given, or how young or ignorant are the children under his care, he needs carefully to consider anew the truth he seeks to impart, to study it in all its various bearings, and to inquire how he may best apply it to his pupils. He needs to have illustrations and examples fresh in his mind, to be a thorough and entire master of his subject, that he may never be at a loss in giving the needed explanation or in imparting the desired knowledge. Where the mind has been chiefly occupied with other duties and distracting cares during the week, this hour of faithful study is especially requisite; for if the teacher resumes the thread of his instruction where it was suspended the week before, with no intervening thought, no higher progress or more definite knowledge on his own part, his resources will very soon be exhausted, to say nothing of the decline of interest in his pupils.

The pastor of one of our long-established churches remarked, not long since, in an address to the teachers of his school, "I think myself authorized to speak on this point with some confidence; for, though I have made the Scriptures my constant and critical study for more than twenty years, yet, were I to attend the exercises of a Sunday-school class, I should not consider myself right and safe in so doing without special preparation for the lesson of the day. . . . . Without such a preparation, the exercise will dwindle into a mere mechanical recitation, or else much of what is said will be crude and undigested, some of it inaccurate, most of it trivial and unsatisfying. . . . . Let your pupil go from you feeling that, in the knowledge of God and of Christ, both in the intellectual and in the heart knowledge, there is not only a life-long work, but that

'A work so vast, a theme so high,
Demands and crowns eternity.'"

Secondly, it is the duty of the teacher to make direct spiritual preparation for meeting his class; that is, the season of instruction should always be preceded by the hour of secret and devout prayer, and prolonged communion with Christ; — not a mere formal act of worship, not a lifeless petition prompted by a sense of duty, the prayer, not of form, but of faith, the soul holding a true and conscious intercourse with the Unseen and Eternal.

A faithful intellectual preparation may seem to be all-sufficient; but such teaching will soon be found, like the shining glaciers of the towering Alps, brilliant and attractive for a brief season, but ever cold. Though the soul may seek to dwell constantly beneath the quickening beams of the Sun of Righteousness, it needs such special seasons to reanimate and to revivify its power, to seek renewedly the baptism of the Holy Spirit, that its whole being may be permeated and filled as with an unction from the Holy One.

It needs to watch in lowly prayer and conscious self-abasement amid the shades and agony of Gethsemane, to bow in deep contrition and penitence before the cross on Calvary, to stand in awe and joyous faith beside the broken sepulchre, to climb in earnest prayer and holy aspiration the glorious mount of ascension. It needs to listen to the inspiring, animating, gentle tones of the Master's voice, to feel the quickening inspiration of his presence, to place the hand confidingly in his, and with unhesitating faith to accept the promise, "My grace is sufficient for thee." It needs to pass through the mere outer courts of the great spiritual temple, to look within the veil, and to enter with reverential awe even into the Holy of Holies; and alone, in that secret sanctuary, through the way consecrated by the great High-Priest and Intercessor, to hold communion with Him, whose presence is no longer visibly manifest in the glory and the cloud, as of old, to the chosen race of Israel, but now far more truly and for ever revealed in the person of the Saviour.

As the teacher thus goes to his Sabbath duties, seemingly so trifling and insignificant, he will feel that he is encompassed by "a great cloud of witnesses"; and although, in the performance of his duties, he may often pass through the valley of humiliation or climb the hill of difficulty, light from the celestial city will shine upon his path, and angelic voices will chant within his soul the inspiring strain, "Come up hither,— even unto Him who has redeemed us through his own blood, and made us kings and priests unto God."

Let, then, some season be sacredly set apart by the teacher for this direct preparation for his duties. While the Sabbath morning hours may often be too short for this work, let the closing hours of the week be thus consecrated. Let the Saturday evening be set apart as a "preparation season," instead of being devoted, as by so many, to any mere passing amusement or social engagement. Would not the instructions and the services of the school and the sanctuary be imparted and received with far greater earnestness and efficacy, if the engrossing cares and duties, the business and the pleasures of the week were sooner laid aside, and a few hours given to holy meditation, to heavenly communion, and to secret prayer, and a brief period devoted to heart preparation for the duties of the Sabbath?

The maxim often quoted as an excuse for the neglect of such seasons of devotion, that "all days are alike," and that "every day is equally a Sabbath," too generally results in ignoring it altogether, and in levelling downward and earthward, rather than heavenward; for the business and occupations of the week are too often made to intrude upon the day of rest, instead of the holy and spiritual influences of the Sabbath flowing through and purifying the stream of earthly care and engrossing duty.

How blessed this "preparation season" to the Christian household, when the toils of the week are ended, when noisy mirth is hushed, and parents and children unite together in anticipation of the duties and pleasures of the coming Sabbath; when mutual help, sympathy, and encouragement are rendered, and a feeling of more devout reverence, a higher aspiration, and a warmer love, are quickened in every soul!

How important the right improvement of this season, too, to those who would not only join in the services of public worship, but who would teach others also of the way of life!

In regard to the use of this, or any period of time, the *Christian* will not look to the example or custom of the world around, but, under a prevalent and constraining sense of his own accountability, with the Bible for his only guide, act with simple reference to his highest spiritual and eternal interests.

Thus acting, he will never fall into any mere selfish or thoughtless routine of life, for He who gave himself a living sacrifice for man will go before him, ever marking out for him the true path in which to tread.

While the teacher seeks, through heavenly communion and sincere prayer, to prepare his own spirit for the duties of the Sabbath, let him not forget to offer, likewise, earnest and devout intercession in behalf of his pupils. Let him remember their peculiar wants, trials, and temptations, and in fervent intercession bear each one in his heart as he bends in supplication. His direct counsels and words of instruction may seem to effect little good; but who knows the secret influences, the strength and help imparted to others, through such seasons of prayer and intercession? Let him ask in faith, nothing wavering, *knowing* that if the petition be sincere it will assuredly be answered in God's good time. Let him ask, even as the little child goes to its parent with its earnest request, trusting, hopeful, believing. Let him not hesitate, let him not tarry in the far-off country, but bring his supplications and intercessions for others to the footstool of redeeming love, with the same assurance in which he offers the petition for personal guidance and a personal blessing. Such intercessions will never be in vain: they will be heard and answered. In the future world, may not the Christian have added to his crown of rejoicing the grateful blessing of those who seemed utterly cold, indifferent, and careless, but for whom his daily and fervent prayers went forth, that the influences of the Spirit might rest upon them, leading them to Christ and to heaven?

The teacher may also exert a beneficial influence over his pupils by sometimes seeking out opportunities of private intercourse with them, by offering the united prayer for strength and heavenly blessing, by supplicating with and for them the help of the Spirit. For why should not the teacher of a class, as well as the pastor of a large flock, unite with those under his care in this sacred duty, and all together enjoy this blessed privilege? Who can estimate the influence of such moments upon the spiritual character of the pupil!

"That might of faith, O Lord! bestow,
Which cannot ask in vain;
Which will not let the angel go
Until the prayer it gain."

At the present time, when so much scepticism abounds upon the whole subject of prayer, — when, by many, the simple faith taught by Christ, "Ask, and ye shall receive," is almost wholly ignored, and metaphysical questions are raised by half-believers upon the efficacy of prayer, and the reality of the blessing brought to the soul in answer to sincere supplication, as being inconsistent with the immutability of the divine counsels and the omniscience of the Eternal, — prayer being thus regarded only as an act of self-excitation by which the soul is brought into a state of higher self-consciousness, — the Christian teacher needs especially to go back to the very oracles of divine truth, and to look deep within his own soul, that he may learn the lesson of a child-like faith and a conscious dependence, — that he may believe the words of Christ when he says, " Whatsoever ye shall ask the Father in my name, he will give it you."

Were such a spirit of prayer prevalent throughout our schools, should we not notice nobler results? Is it not the *lack of this* more than all things else that so often renders our endeavors void and fruitless? Do we habitually pray, as if we really believed that God is both able and willing to pour forth the quickening influences of his Spirit upon our churches and our schools, — to impart larger measures of life and holiness? Do we pray that they may, indeed, be baptized with the power of the Spirit, aroused to holier endeavors, and filled with a divine energy? Only let such a spirit be kindled among us, let such earnest and fervent supplications go forth from the heart of every teacher, both in behalf of his own pupils and of all our schools, a new impulse and an ever-increasing activity and power of usefulness will be diffused among us, and Christ will be felt to abide with us, as the ever-present Sustainer, Comforter, and Guide.

It is the duty of the teacher to attend, if possible, the regular social meetings, appointed monthly, or at other stated intervals of time, in the school with which he is connected. He should feel the obligation to do all in his power to render such meetings improving and interesting; not putting off all the work upon others, not feeling that the pastor and superintendent are the only ones to render the hour one of mutual benefit, but feeling that he has a part to do, a work to perform, in preparing himself, by reading or reflection, on the given subject of the evening, and so far as he may in imparting the results of his own study or experience, either by writing or conversation. Such meetings, if judiciously conducted, are of essential importance in bringing the teachers together, in creating and sustaining a feeling of mutual interest and sympathy, and in imparting mutual aid and encouragement. Whatever may be regarded by individual schools as the best course to be pursued at such times, whether the direct study of the Scriptures, or the discussion of doctrines or abstract truths, or of questions relating to the immediate welfare of the school, the ultimate end should be one and the same, namely, the improvement and progress of teachers, and through them the advancement of the school, — the meeting together for united prayer and supplication for the help and guidance of the Spirit.

Where this end is lost sight of, where frivolous

conversation or unedifying debate, or mere indifference characterizes the hour, it would be better to give up such meetings at once. If conducted in a serious, devout, yet cheerful spirit, they may be made one of the most fruitful means of a higher and quickened life, and of a deeper interest and closer sympathy among the teachers.

A course has been pursued in some of our long-established schools, and with success, of having a course of study, or a list of subjects of discussion, marked out at the commencement of the season, to be taken up in regular order, a copy of which is furnished to each teacher at the first meeting, by which means he has ample time to read or think upon the subject before it is brought before the meeting for general conversation or discussion. Written communications are requested from any able and willing thus to contribute to the interest of the hour, and the reading of them is followed by more general debate, or private conversation. At other times it may be found more profitable to have the hour devoted to the direct study of the Scriptures.

We need, also, to meet together, that we may *learn to teach;* that those who have just undertaken the duties of the teacher may gather wisdom from the experience of others long and successfully engaged in the work. We have our normal schools to impart the art of teaching to those who would themselves be the instructors of others, in secular truth and scientific knowledge; and equally do we need in the Sabbath school, to embrace every opportunity of progressing, of learning how we may teach better and more truly, how our instructions may be rendered more useful, thorough, and interesting. Above all, let such meetings be sanctified by prayer, and hallowed by devout and earnest supplication. Whatever may be the discussions or the teachings of the hour, let there be the united intercessions for divine help and blessing; for the conscious guidance, the renewing and sanctifying influences of the Spirit, thus fulfilling the Saviour's prayer, "That they all may be one, as thou, Father, art in me, and I in thee, that they may be one in us."

Another direct and important duty of the teacher is to become acquainted with his pupils in their own homes; to learn the influences which there surround them; the dangers and temptations to which they may be exposed; their peculiar trials, wants, difficulties, and opportunities. Where such intercourse is seconded by the interest and co-operation of parents, a means of influence is opened which cannot be over-estimated. Here we are met by a difficulty, which, to many, is not slight nor imaginary. In many of our schools, the children of a class move in a different, and so-called higher social circle than the teacher; and naturally there is a conscious diffidence or backwardness on his or her part in taking the first step toward such a mutual acquaintance.

We have known pupils remain under the care of the same teacher for four or five years, and yet the parents make no advance toward such intercourse; never express any word of encouragement or indebtedness to the teacher, or evince the least interest in the studies of their children or the welfare of the school.

What a chilling and depressing influence such indifference has upon a sensitive heart few but the individual can know. Never will our schools take their true position, and become the means of a high spiritual nurture, until parents more generally manifest a direct, personal interest in their improvement and success. Some expression of interest is due to the faithful teacher; and though he may be able and willing to labor perseveringly and prayerfully from the highest of motives, how much would a few words of encouragement and interest often do to lighten his labors, and to cheer him in his work!

On the other hand, let the teacher be faithful to his own duties, in visiting his pupils from time to time, whenever such intercourse is possible, — especially in cases of sickness or peculiar trial. If they are in poverty or want, let him lend the helping hand, or give the word of encouragement; if in suffering, speak the word of a heart-felt sympathy; if in sorrow, mourn with them. Let him evince, by every means in his power, that his interest is not confined to the Sabbath hour. Let him direct their reading, if they have no truer and better guide at home; let him sometimes seek with them the beautiful haunts of nature, and by cheerful conversation lead their thoughts and aspirations to the great and good Giver of all; let him go with them occasionally to the dwellings of poverty or suffering, and teach them the blessings of an active charity and a true thoughtfulness for others, and point out to them in what simple ways they may be useful to others, however limited their means or opportunities.

Let him occasionally seek to deepen their good resolutions, or point out some particular fault, by a simple note; for even if the child be so young as to require it to be printed, it will often have a deeper and more lasting influence, will touch the heart more truly, than any regular lesson. With the older pupils, how often, through the medium of a letter, will a kind remonstrance, or an earnest plea for a higher spiritual life, for self-consecration to Christ, be more efficacious than any spoken words!

Let him endeavor to awaken or to increase the interest of his pupils in the public services of religion; to deepen their reverence for the sanctuary and their attachment to the Church. Let the immediate subject of the services be often referred to, and made a topic of conversation in the class, and let even the younger children be taught to pay attention to the reading of the Scriptures and the hymns, though the sermon itself may be above their comprehension.

Above all, let the teacher feel it to be his *own* duty to be a punctual and regular attendant upon the services of public worship. Let not his practice contradict his teachings, nor his example belie his words. Let the pupil see, that to him, at least, the Sabbath, with all its blessed influences, its means of instruction, its opportunities of improvement, its meetings for solemn worship and devout prayer, is a holy season, a season of religious privilege, a season for religious thought and spiritual communion, marked by no austerity nor gloom, but cheerful and happy.

Let not his seat in the sanctuary be found vacant with every cloud in the sky, every cold winter's wind, or warm summer's breeze; but let him prove that he so far values such privileges as occasionally to make some little exertion, or practise a little self-denial, in order to be present at the regular service.

A teacher who instructs his class in the morning, and spends the afternoon in walking, riding, or visiting, or lounges at home reading the newspaper or the last new novel, will exert but a dubious influence on his pupils. Actions speak louder than words, and their influence is more enduring. Character possesses an unmeasured power and an all-potent influence, though no direct word of counsel or rebuke be uttered; but mere teaching, unless the life in some good degree correspond, is worse than useless.

While there exists such a growing indifference to the institutions of religion, while the great interests of public worship are made to depend chiefly upon the peculiar talent or fidelity of one individual, so that if he be removed, the church often degenerates at once, as if its whole life were concentrated in one person, instead of being an active, vital principle, diffused through every limb of the whole body, self-sustained and life-diffusing; — while nice criticisms upon the style or manner of the preacher are made to take the place of a self-application of the truths uttered; while a brilliant intellect is so often preferred to a profound, realizing faith, or a fine theoretical discussion excites a deeper interest than the simple, solemn utterance of divine, eternal truths; — the teacher needs firmly and definitely to take his only true position; to manifest, by a devout and reverential observance of the public services of the Sabbath, that he regards them as of importance, and to evince, both by word and action, that the great object of such worship is, not the mere hearing of this or that favorite preacher, but the worship of God, and the promotion of the soul's spiritual and eternal good.

These and other duties might easily be enlarged upon; but the conscientious teacher will never be left in darkness as to the true path of duty and of effort.

Looking unto Jesus, — seeking, through daily prayer, Divine help, — waiting on the Spirit, — he will ever seek higher aims and wider views of truth and of duty, remembering that Divine promise: "Be thou faithful unto death, and I will give thee a crown of life."

> "No act falls fruitless; none can tell
> How vast its power may be;
> Nor what results, enfolded, dwell
> Within it silently.
>
> "Work on; despair not; bring thy mite,
> Nor care how small it be;
> God is with all who serve the right,
> The holy, true, and free."

CHAPTER IX.

CLASSIFICATION OF PUPILS.—USE OF MANUALS, &C.

"Not in proud and lofty dreaming,
But in glowing, active zeal,
Humbly its own worth esteeming
Laboring still for human weal;
Christian! shall to thee be given,
Wisdom, grace, the love of heaven."

It is sometimes remarked, and with a degree of truth, that, much as has been written and said on the Sunday school, frequent as are the public meetings for debate and discussion on its true modes of operation, and its legitimate aim and object, the practical question, "What am I to do?" often remains unanswered, as the teacher turns to the immediate duties of his class.

We shall endeavor, therefore, in the present chapter, to give a few brief hints on the manner in which a more systematic arrangement of classes may be introduced, and to offer a few simple suggestions on the mode of instructing the youngest pupils, considering in brief the true use of manuals and text-books, as aids in the study of the Bible.

The first requisite for any permanent and real improvement, either in the single class or in the school collectively, we have already shown to consist in the true spiritual and intellectual preparation of the teacher for his work.

The next point to which we would advert, is the better classification of the school. We are aware that on this point it is easier to theorize than to practise; yet we believe, that with some definite, determined aim in view, much even here may be accomplished. To feel the want is the first step towards improvement. Each individual class, with the exception, perhaps, of those composed of the very youngest children, should be engaged on the same lesson; and to this end, children will be classed of course according to their capabilities and progress,and not according to age. To have the single hour — often only an half-hour — reserved for direct instruction in the classes divided among two, three, and even four recitations, must of course render each either very brief or very superficial, and will strengthen in the pupil the too prevalent idea that a mere cursory knowledge of the Bible, or a lesson repeated memoriter, is all that is essential.

One hour a week, with those teachers who are so fortunate as to obtain such a length of time for class instruction, is surely brief enough to speak of themes so vast and so momentous as are revealed in both the old and new dispensations of truth, to enlarge on their rich lessons of biography and history, their stores of poetry and prophecy, their words of warning and retribution, and their promises of hope and eternal blessedness.

When a pupil enters the school, let it be the duty of the superintendent to converse freely with him, to examine him in his knowledge of the Scriptures, to ascertain something of his home life, and of his character and disposition, and then to place him, with the consent of the teacher, in such a class as seems best suited to his needs and capacities; and if, after a few weeks, there are good reasons for making a change, some other and permanent teacher may be found. It is said, " Supposing a teacher commences with a class of six pupils, of average capacity and advancement, and with the intention of keeping them together as long as possible. Within one or two years, perhaps half of them, from various causes, have left the school; their parents have removed to other towns or cities, or sickness has obliged them to remain at home. How, then, is the teacher to supply their place? for he is unwilling to give up those still remaining with him, to whom he has already become strongly attached." In such a case, some teachers take children much younger into their classes, to commence leading them on, as those who have left; but this, of course, creates a division in the class, and limits the time to be devoted to each portion.

Would it not be much better, in almost every case, to supply such vacancies by pupils able to unite with the original members of the class, and so to continue in the same course of instruction? Such a method possesses many advantages, and a little attention on the part of superintendents and teachers could easily secure the desired end. To have well-informed pupils of fifteen or sixteen years of age in the same class with children of six or seven seems utterly incongruous, and a mode of classification which would never be tolerated in our day-schools. Are we not, in so doing, limiting our means of usefulness, and curtailing the brief opportunities we now possess of imparting instruction in spiritual truth?

Some teachers are peculiarly fitted to interest the youngest pupils, and by a winning, gentle manner, can secure order, attention, and interest, without any word of authority; while others as naturally seek those more advanced, whose lessons require more direct study and thought. Judgment and observation are, therefore, needed in classifying any school; but let not mere caprice, on the part either of the teacher or of the pupil, justify a change of classes; let not vant of perseverance or faith be concealed under plea of want of ability, or a mere desire of hange be deemed a sufficient excuse.

The ties formed between the true teacher and is pupils are too sacred and strong to be lightly r wantonly sundered, and the spiritual influence vhich he exerts over them is to be regarded be-ore all things else. If the good of the pupil de-nand a change of classes, such change should e made, and a course of regular, systematic in-truction pursued.

To mark out the same exact course for all he pupils in the school, where they possess o widely different advantages, and occupy so ifferent positions in life, and remain in the chool for such different periods of time, is im-ossible. If some distinct, definite plan is clearly aid down, and fully understood by the teachers, vhich they shall feel bound to follow out as far s possible, we believe that it will be essentially etter and more practicable to leave the details of he plan to the judgment of the individual eachers, than to attempt any rigid enforcement. his, of course, throws a greater responsibility on e teacher; but such a responsibility to any ctive, earnest mind will be quickening rather an depressing. He will not regard himself as mere machine, but as an essential limb of the hole body; and any change he may make in is class, or in his course of instruction, will not be done without thought and prayer, and reference to the ultimate good of the pupil.

It is often asked, How are the younger pupils to be instructed and interested? A partial answer to this question may be found in what has already been said; but as a more direct reply, we would offer a few brief hints. Let the youngest child have some definite lesson to prepare, however short or simple; let him commit one or more verses of a hymn, or a short passage of Scripture, previously explained, and then let the teacher illustrate the lesson by direct and simple conversation. The remainder of the hour may be profitably occupied by the teacher's reading some portion of Scripture, some story from the Old Testament, or an account of some one of Christ's miracles, or a parable from the New Testament, and explaining as he reads; and, on the following Sabbath, requiring the children to give an account of what was read the previous week, and questioning them, to ascertain the correctness of their knowledge. In this way, a very young child may be made familiar with all the leading narratives of the Scriptures; and where little home instruction is given, such lessons will be found more attractive than almost anything else; for the insatiable craving of children for "stories" will seldom be wearied with those of Joseph and Moses, of Samuel and David, of Elijah and Daniel. With such a ımentable deficiency as now exists of any ac-urate knowledge of the Old-Testament history nd biography, how can the want be better rem-died, than by interesting the young mind in ts rich stores of instruction? The child will ·ever forget the impressions thus received, and owever great his subsequent acquirements, he vill never outgrow his interest in these conse-rated records of an early age, — in the strange nd wonderful history of the chosen people of ehovah. With such a foundation, when the hild commences the direct study of either the Old or the New Testament, with the use of some nanual, he will have a stock of information on vhich to fall back, and will find his lessons of louble interest. The amount of good that might e gained by the faithful use of home opportu-ities in this way can hardly be overestimated. f parents or elder brothers and sisters felt the esponsibility of thus interesting the younger nembers of the home circle in the wonderful ecords of the Bible, far less need would there be o deplore, as we do now, the strange ignorance f its contents even among those well informed n other topics.

The mere reading of the Bible in course, from Genesis to Revelation, as if this alone were a natter of comment or praise in the child or youth, s, we hardly need say, a useless practice. Let selections be pointed out to him, to read by himself, or passages read aloud and explained t· him, and he will never look on the Bible as : "dull book," or a book only for Sundays. Her we would record our remonstrance against th practice, common in some schools, of occupyin; the brief hour of instruction in reading to th younger children mere story-books or tales fro a child's paper. Occasionally, this may be don to advantage; but to lay the Bible aside, as i the child were too young to understand its les sons of divine truth, and to supplant it by som feeble, trifling fiction, is utterly unworthy th great object of Sunday-school tuition. Wit the younger and the elder pupils, let the Bible and the Bible alone, be the chief book of instruc tion. Manuals are of value only as they hel to illustrate and unfold the truth of the divin record; and are not those to be regarded as es sentially deficient which do not direct the pupi to search, for himself, the records of Revelation The manual is only of secondary importance, to give point and definiteness to the lesson, an to let the pupil have something to do in preparin for the exercises of the school.

The *faithful* teacher will never bound his in struction by a given number of questions an answers; for he will feel that such a recitation i but a poor fulfilment of his duties.

"It is little trouble to have charge of a class now," said a teacher in one of our city schools not long since; "for, with a regular series of books to use, we have nothing to do but just to ask the questions, and be sure that the right answers are given." On being asked if she did not make it a practice to converse with her pupils, or to study the lesson by herself, she replied, "O, no! The answers and the references given I presume are all correct; and then we have but just time to go through the regular lesson before the school closes."

Is there not too much of this kind of instruction, if it deserves to be called such, even in our best schools? A manual, at the best, is only suggestive, and should be used by the teacher always as a means, not as an end; and should ever be regarded as a help to the study of the Bible, and as subsidiary to the direct examination of its pages. The old-fashioned custom, if so it may be called, of committing to memory portions of the Scriptures and hymns, is one which ought not to be discontinued among our pupils. The stores of sacred truth thus laid up in the mind are invaluable treasures in after years; and what poetry more sublime, what strains more elevating, than the inspired rhythm of psalmist and prophet? It is well known how long the verses and hymns, committed in childhood, remain fixed in the memory, when all things else fade and are forgotten; but why should this practice be confined, as is usually the case, to the very youngest members of a school? There are surely stores enough of sublime poetry, of devout prayer, and of solemn praise, embracing the richest treasures for those of older years, and of inestimable value to be laid up in the memory; and, with the assistance of the teacher, such selections could easily be made, and could constitute a part of the regular recitations of the class.

Every child should commit to memory the Commandments, the Lord's Prayer, and some simple form of morning and evening devotion, suitable to express his peculiar desires and needs; for to those, especially, wholly destitute of home religious instruction and influence, such forms are invaluable helps in the promotion of a religious spirit and the growth of the Christian character. Often will they dwell in the mind, when mere words of counsel or admonition are forgotten, and form an effective barrier against sudden temptation or fierce passion. At the same time, let the spirit of prayer and devotion be so inculcated that the child shall soon be led to express his wants and to proffer his petitions in his own words, however childlike and simple.

We are sometimes told that the pupils have no time to prepare their lessons; that their school duties through the week occupy all their hours; and that they need Sunday as a day of rest and relaxation. If this be truly the case, we would say emphatically, Let some or all other studies be given up, rather than that of the Bible; for which is of the most lasting consequence, a French or a Latin verb and a problem of Euclid, or a knowledge of Gospel truth? There is a fitting time and an appropriate season for each and for all; but where such studies are made to encroach on the Sabbath, or the weariness resulting from them, in any one case, prevents the desire for spiritual instruction and preparation for the duties of the school and sanctuary, there is something radically wrong in the system of education, and parents are solemnly responsible for the result. Let the child and the youth be taught that there are some studies and some courses of reading peculiarly appropriate to the sacredness of the Sabbath, and that his grammar and arithmetic and algebra are then to be laid aside. Let works illustrative of Bible truth, the rich stores of Christian biography, the history of the wonderful fortunes of the Jewish race, works of sacred poetry, and such as point out the marks of the Creator's wisdom, power, and love in all the beautiful forms of nature, — let all such be freely opened to the child; for they will minister to his spiritual wants and desires, while they contribute also to his intellectual growth.

There is a knowledge to be gained of the establishment and progress of Christianity in the world, the evidences of the truth of revealed religion, and an acquaintance with the leading parties and sects of the Church, — all offering a wide range for individual taste and preference, in those of maturer years.

If our pupils are to become the future teachers of these schools, is it not of vast importance that they should be well informed on these and kindred subjects?

That the teacher should possess definite and clear ideas of the truth he teaches has already been considered; and of equal consequence is it, that, as the pupil leaves the school, he should know distinctly *what* he believes. Lessons, therefore, on Christian doctrine, not controversial or bigoted, should form a distinct part of the course of studies pursued; for unless the youth possesses some definite knowledge of the leading truths of the faith in which he believes, he will become a ready prey to the shafts of scepticism or to the sneers of ridicule. Let such truths be distinctly fixed in his mind, and however few or simple, they will be the living germ of a growing and enlarged faith, the sure foundation of the belief and trust of future years.

Amid the various perplexing questions that arise from time to time in every school, the teacher may sometimes feel discouraged and uncertain as to the best mode of action. True, mistakes have been, and will again be made, and we shall sometimes find the right path only after long and devious wanderings. Let no individual feel that he is exempt from doing his part, however trifling, towards the introduction of a better system and of a higher order of teaching in our schools. Laborers of every capacity, if only faithful, are needed in the building up of the one great spiritual Temple. Only let its foundations be laid in faith, and its walls consecrated by prayer and heavenly communion, and its work wrought in a sense of entire dependence upon God, and in his own time it will rise in fair and beautiful proportions, a meet dwelling for the Holy Spirit.

CHAPTER X.

ORDER AND METHOD. — SUNDAY-SCHOOL LIBRARIES.

"No existence is commonplace to him who lives with uncommon aims. The meanest work, carried on with insight and hope, with a feeling of the beautiful and with reference to the whole of which we are parts, becomes large and important."

THERE is no point on which the thorough and hearty co-operation of individual teachers is more essential, in order to render the short time devoted to Sunday-school instruction conducive to the best results, than the enforcing and maintaining of the most entire order and regularity in all its duties and exercises.

Children of all ages and capacities are brought together, some of whom have never been subjected to any authority or restraint at home; while others are prone to take advantage of the absence of any penal discipline in the school, and to make the hour one of amusement and recreation rather than of improvement; and unless there is a distinct understanding among the teachers of the necessity of individual firmness in the government of their respective classes, of the necessity of maintaining the most entire *order* and *regularity*, and infusing as far as possible a spirit of *reverence* among the pupils, the school will degenerate at once.

Where this is not the case, where, as in too many schools, amusement is made paramount to instruction, and order sacrificed to the caprice of the passing moment, a most grievous wrong is done to the spiritual nature of all concerned. Amusement, laughter, or trifling conversation among the pupils, whispering among the teachers, lessons recited as a mere form, and often followed by an address with no point, no definite aim, as if the speaker felt that he was conferring an obligation in saying something, no matter what or how trifling, a hasty dismission and a hurried exit, — such a school, or one in any way resembling such, is worse, — we speak deliberately, — infinitely worse than the entire absence of religious instruction. Religion is degraded, truth dethroned, and Christ crucified anew. Let a child have no religious instruction, let him be debarred, by early want and disadvantage, from the public teachings of the Sabbath, and we would gladly believe that in the Father's all-embracing love such a soul might be so influenced by the secret monitions of the Spirit, that the germs of a true spiritual life would be quickened, and expand in full and beautiful unfoldings in the genial light of the heavenly land, beneath the Saviour's tender guardianship.

Let the child enter a school that is characterized by disorder and frivolity, let him be placed under the charge of a teacher who has no vital sense of the infinite moment of his work, and the germs of religious sensibility are soon crushed, the conscience is deadened, the interest flags, faith grows dim and dies, and religion becomes a mere ceremony, without any living spirit: the present is all, and eternity and retribution, and Christ and heaven, are mere barren fantasies. Even in a school where the general regulations are orderly and systematic, and the exercises devout and serious, if the child receive direct instruction from a teacher whom he knows to be worldly, frivolous, and careless, the same effect will more than probably result in that individual case.

Let the child be blessed by religious home influences, and such results may in part be counteracted, but never wholly; the after life, if rightly directed, must be a struggle to overcome such early impressions: and how hard that struggle few, save the individual himself, can tell.

Is it asked, What, then, is to be done? We answer emphatically, Insist on order, method, discipline, in the general government of the school, and in individual classes; and, if this cannot be had by the use of firm and judicious means, let the school be closed at once. Nothing can be effected worthy of a Christian school without order. The sooner an ill-managed, ill-regulated, ill-governed school is disbanded, the better.

That order and discipline *can* be maintained without any direct show of authority, and seriousness and reverence characterize the hour, we well know. Much, very much, depends on the character of the superintendent, and the judicious authority which he may exercise in the general oversight of the school. But let him possess the very best intentions, and strive to the utmost to enforce the regulations of the school, and it will avail little, unless each teacher feels his own individual responsibility in co-operating with him.

Let a few plain, simple regulations be made for the use of the school, according to its peculiar wants and individual necessities, and let each teacher as he enters upon his duties be furnished with a copy of the same, with the distinct understanding that he is bound to carry them out in the government of his own class, and by his example to assist in the enforcement of them in the school at large. Let there be method in the entire arrangement of the general exercises of the school; in registering the names of pupils and teachers; in keeping an account of the average attendance, and the transfer of pupils from one class to another; in the distribution of books, the manner of opening and closing the school, &c.; though on these and kindred topics, of course, each school must make its own regulations. Only let not the rules remain as mere dead letters on the statute-books, as if such belonged to a period less advanced, or, as some imagine, less spiritual, than our own. Put life into them. Make them effective and vital; for it is only through such system and order, vainly denominated by some "mere mechanical forms," that we can ever attain the highest and truest spiritual results.

Much might be done to promote this end, by a more faithful punctuality on the part of both teachers and pupils; but having already spoken on this point, we would refer to what constitutes a great interruption, and creates much disorder in many even of our best-regulated schools; namely, the distribution and exchange of library books among the pupils. If it is necessary that this should be done on the Sabbath, we would have the library opened before the commencement of the school, so that a selection of books may be made by the teachers, without occupying any of the time set apart for the exercises of the school. When the school is about to be dismissed, let the children receive to take home with them such books as the teacher sees fit.

The teacher should always be acquainted with

the character and contents of the books he selects, and choose such as are appropriate to the child's age and capacity; letting him understand distinctly that he is personally responsible for the good use and safe-keeping of the same. Another regulation, adopted in some schools, and which might with little effort be easily carried out in almost all, seems to us much more conducive to the good order of the school. Let the library be opened at a certain hour during the week, and then let the teacher go and make such selections as he knows his class most needs, — placing the books with the manuals or service-books used by the pupils, and then, on the following Sunday, simply exchanging them with those returned by the children, charging the number of each volume to the individual by whom it is received. The teacher would not be obliged to visit the library more than once in several weeks, as the different pupils in his class would receive in turn the books selected, some, of course, keeping them longer than a single week.

This method prevents all confusion in the school, — the constant leaving of seats by either teachers or pupils, the looking over of miscellaneous volumes to find such as might be suitable, and the expenditure of time too valuable to be spared from the direct instructions of the school.

In the treatment of the library, much depends

on the librarian's habits of method and order, and on his accuracy and fidelity in the care of the books; but equally essential is it that each teacher should co-operate in the rigid enforcement of all the regulations of the library; for only in this way is it possible to secure the good use and the safe-keeping of the books.

Is not something more needed in most of our schools than improvement in the merely external arrangements of the library? Do we not greatly need a higher order of books, — books that will at once interest children and contribute to the growth of their intellectual and moral powers, without creating a morbid love for mere works of fiction, which soon leads to an utter distaste for all but novel-reading and the light literature of the day? Is not much of the prevalent superficiality and the want of intellectual vigor in many of those just entering on mature life attributable to the habits of desultory reading, and the thirst for exciting mental stimulants acquired during the period of childhood?

We would not, by any means, exclude from our libraries all works of fiction; but they should constitute only the minor portion of the books, and should be such as directly to enforce high moral lessons. To admit every book, however trite its aim or weak its style, simply because "the good child is rewarded, and the disobedient punished," — an effect, by the way, not always to be seen in real life, — seems to us unworthy the true aim of such libraries, and the high moral tone and influence that should flow from the Sunday school.

Much as is often said of the superior advantages enjoyed by the children of the present age, we have sometimes thought, when looking over the well-filled shelves of juvenile libraries, embracing miniature biographies and histories, and stories without end, that some of those of the past generation, whose only recreation was to be found in Plutarch and Rollin, stood a better chance of possessing a vigorous and active mind, and powers capable of exertion, than very many of the youth of the present time.

The child is often praised for his fondness for his books, and his love of reading; but give him a book that requires some attention and thought, one that will really prove of service and use to him, and generally, though fully adapted to his capacities, it will soon be laid aside as wearisome and uninteresting. The teacher soon discovers this, in the selections he makes for his class, and when the pupil has read through the story-books contained in the library, its interest is exhausted.

Is not some decided improvement needed?

That parents are, first and chief of all, solemnly responsible for the mental habits and moral tastes of their children few will deny; yet how few comparatively take any interest in the subject, or ever inquire what the child is reading, so long as he is only quiet, and makes no interruption! How few ever question the child on what he has read, or make it an object to ascertain if the hours thus passed are of any real, lasting benefit to him! The free access which many children possess to a common circulating library has a most baneful effect on their whole moral and intellectual well-being. We have known those whose parents were well able, both from education and position, to instruct and direct their children, allowed to select books entirely at random; and often have we seen children of ten and twelve years of age, and even younger, freely reading the emptiest novels, and such as had a most doubtful moral bearing.

What results must necessarily follow? The taste becomes vitiated, the moral perceptions blunted, the conscience hardened by constant familiarity with scenes of a low and unworthy character, from which the child would be carefully excluded in real life, and a craving for constant excitement fostered, until every-day duties and definite studies become altogether tame and uninteresting, and by slow but sure degrees the health of the mind is destroyed, and its purity for ever lost.

Great as is the responsibility of parents, are not Sunday-school teachers in a measure accountable for the intellectual tastes and habits of their pupils? Ought not our libraries to embrace works of more substantial value than are now to be found in many or most of them? and should not the teacher make it a more definite aim to select such books as will really benefit the child?

Only create a demand for books of a higher order than such as now usually fill the shelves of our juvenile libraries, and it will be met. There is talent and power and efficiency enough among us to answer every call for a more extended usefulness, if it only be directed in the right channel, if the ruling and fundamental aim be only determined, lofty, and true.

Subjects of this kind may seem trite and insignificant. They are not so, when viewed in connection with their true and legitimate results. The humblest deed, if wrought in the spirit of Christ, becomes large and divine; and in no office more than in that of the Christian teacher do we need the true spirit of individual fidelity and of personal responsibility to God and to Christ, — the spirit of abiding trust, and of a vital, hopeful faith, united with a distinct and definite aim for personal improvement; for such a spirit, and this only, will react on the whole body of our schools, and render them effective agencies for a higher spiritual nurture.

CHAPTER XI.

THE OBSERVANCE OF THE LORD'S SUPPER.

" Gethsemane can I forget,
Or there thy conflict see,
Thine agony and bloody sweat,
And not remember thee ?

" When to the cross I turn mine eye,
And rest on Calvary,
O Lamb of God, my sacrifice!
I must remember thee! "

WE have already considered, more or less in detail, the essential qualifications of the religious teacher, and the duties which he owes both to himself and his pupils. There remains still another class of duties and obligations really embraced within these, but which from its very nature requires separate consideration, namely, the relation of the teacher to the Church of Christ.

It is not uncommon to meet the individual who regards this relation as one entirely at the option of his own inclination, — one which he may assume or ignore at pleasure, and which brings with it no peculiar responsibilities or privileges. He regards the Church as a sort of abstraction, having no vital connection with his own spiritual welfare; as something essential, indeed, to the promotion of Christianity, but with which he has little or nothing to do. He regards its interests as belonging to a chosen few, and feels that so long as he leads a correct and upright life, so long as his moral character is irreproachable, and he is active in the duties of benevolence and charity, he is exempt from all further obligation.

The Apostle's sublime thought, of all true hearted believers forming one perfect spiritual body, of which Christ is the head, — his spirit flowing through and quickening each individual member, and imparting life, strength, and vigor to each separate limb, without which none could perform its appointed functions, is regarded as a sort of fanciful chimera, never actually to be realized through individual growth and a personal union with the divine Saviour.

The idea of any distinct, open, fearless choice to be made between the two great forces that even now divide the entire moral universe is one wholly lost sight of in much of the teaching of the present day; and many rest satisfied with a low standard, a tame mediocrity, and a languid piety, as if somehow all would be well with them in the end, and as if God were altogether too merciful to reject any so good as themselves, though their virtue is only that of outward surroundings, though they have known no inward renewal, and have been conscious of no close, personal relationship to God and to Christ.

Were the Christian Church to have war waged upon it from without, as in the earlier days of its establishment, or were it possible to have some decisive proof by which the genuineness of a living faith might be tested, we should witness a stranger division now within its borders, among those nominally Christians, than has ever been created by the conflicts of creed, sect, or party.

Go into any of our Sabbath schools, and how many do we find engaged as teachers who have never distinctly recognized their individual indebtedness to Christ, and who feel that they have no individual union with his Church! Is there not something utterly incongruous, to say the least, in acknowledging the importance of Christ's teachings and mission, so far as to be desirous of imparting the truths of his Gospel to others, and yet feeling no obligation to fulfil his last and dying request, or in any direct form to become a living, active member of the Church, which is His body? Is there not prevalent a strange and mistaken feeling on this whole subject? Which, indeed, abstractly considered, is the most solemn and responsible act, to commune with the Saviour at his table, a service individual in its very nature, or to seek to impart to other spirits the eternal truths of God, to utter words that shall have an undying influence over immortal souls? Is it a more direct profession of faith in Christ, to obey his parting command, "This do in remembrance of me," than to gather the lambs of his flock, and to teach them of the one good Shepherd? Why should the office of the Christian teacher be one so lightly assumed, regarded as open to the most inexperienced, considered too often as embracing no peculiar obligations, and yet the two simple rites by which the individual recognizes his relation to the Church, or brings himself into a more intimate union with this or that particular organization of some portion of the Church, be so much neglected, as if some far higher obligation, some far more weighty responsibility were then incurred? Is there not a radical defect in the general mind on the relative importance of these subjects? Have we not substituted a law and a standard of our own for that of the Gospel?

If the individual be really unfit to unite in the sacred service of commemoration, if he have no affection for Christ, no sense of indebtedness to him, no conscious need of a Saviour, then he is equally unfit to be a teacher of divine truths to others.

On the other hand, if he so feels the solemn

realities of life, the love of God, and his own obligations as a steward of the divine bounty, as to desire and pray to be God's minister of good to others, then he ought to confirm this desire, and strengthen this prayer, by an open acknowledgment of the Saviour's claims upon his gratitude and love.

It is said, that many are really desirous of doing good to others, and are conscientious in the performance of their duties as teachers, who yet feel that they are not "good enough" to commune with their Saviour. Whenever this excuse is *conscientiously* given, we cannot but feel that it forms one strong reason why the individual should be the more strongly urged gladly and freely to unite in this simple service; for it is the humble, the self-distrustful, the watchful disciple who bears the nearest kindred to his Master. As these words are usually uttered, they imply an utterly wrong state of feeling, as if a certain amount of goodness, a certain degree of merit, were essential to recommend one to the divine favor. The too prevalent feeling, and one which secretly mars the symmetry of many an otherwise Christ-like character, that what we *do* possesses a sort of inherent efficacy in meriting the approval of God, is one that needs to be distinctly encountered both in the preaching and the teaching of the present day. Outward duties and benevolent organizations are substituted for inward communion and heavenly aspiration, and deeds of charity are too often made to take the place of a living heart-faith in Christ. So the idea gains a yet stronger hold, that such works may be performed, and such duties engaged in, without any deep, abiding faith, as if such poor deeds alone could place the soul in a state of acceptance and reconciliation with God.

Among all the excuses usually offered for the neglect of this beautiful service of commemoration, — that its observance was only binding upon the early disciples, that no visible good results from it, that the individual is not good enough to take so decided a stand, that he does not want to set himself up as an example, that he is too diffident to profess so openly his faith before others, and many other reasons, only too familiar to the faithful pastor or teacher, — there is yet one, seldom urged, but which lies at the very foundation of all others, and which, though often unacknowledged by the individual, is really the secret cause of all his hesitancy, doubt, and lack of interest, namely, the want of a true love to Christ, and of a sense of personal indebtedness to him.

If this be in the soul, — if the deep sense of unworthiness, the conviction of sin, the dread consciousness of a holy and violated law, have been followed by peace and reconciliation through a crucified Saviour; if gratitude and trust have succeeded the tears of penitence and remorse, and a child-like faith in a Father's mercy, in the consciousness of what Christ has done and is still doing for the soul, fills the spirit with a quiet confidence, — then will it no longer hesitate. Its ruling desire and earnest aim will be, to show forth in the fullest and clearest manner its heart-felt love. The whole life will be the constant expression of its deep indebtedness, and it will joyfully hasten to acknowledge, in the commemoration of its Saviour in the way of his own appointment, its personal gratitude and love. No fear of human censure or ridicule, no thought of man, will then stand between the soul and its Redeemer.

> " 'T is love, 't is love; Thou diedst for me!
>   I hear thy whisper in my heart;
> The morning breaks; the shadows flee:
>   Pure, universal Love thou art!
> My prayer hath power with God! the grace
>   Unspeakable I now receive.
> In vain I have not wept and strove;
>   Thy nature and thy name is Love!"

This conviction of sin and unworthiness, this need of pardon and reconciliation, this love to Jesus, comes not to the soul as of itself, undesired and unprayed for. It comes not amid the press of business, the search for amusement, the mere mechanical routine of duty, but only through the sacred ministries of silence and solitude and self-recollection, through the holy influence of prayer and divine communion.

Thus it becomes evident where alone we may find a church or a school that is really alive and vital. "It is only where the reconciling office of Christ is felt as a reality, and where the immediate gifts of his divine spirit in the communion of love are a part of the soul's experience." If such be realized by the Christian teacher, if he has learned something of the soul's deeper experiences, and of his own utter weakness and inability unless he seek indeed to *abide* in Christ, then, as he enters on his duties as a guide to others, he will also openly acknowledge his faith in the Redeemer, and gladly sit at his Master's table, fulfilling his last and dying request, "This do in remembrance of me."

Some may ask, "Are not new and solemn responsibilities incurred by those who thus take upon themselves their Redeemer's covenant?" We reply, None that are not equally binding upon all who claim for themselves the name of *Christian.* To acknowledge, either directly or indirectly, Christ as the soul's guide, leader, and example, is to acknowledge the highest standard of character, the strictest rule of self-judgment. To neglect the observance of this simple yet comprehensive ordinance, established by the Saviour himself in an hour for ever consecrated to the Christian heart, and hallowed by the observance of ages, is not merely to neglect the command of the Master, but to slight the dying request of Him whose love was stronger than death, through whom alone we have the assurance of pardon and acceptance. But let not this rite ever be regarded as an end, as an expression of some definite attainment in goodness; for if so, what conscientious heart would ever participate in it? No: it is simply an expression of personal attachment to the Saviour, of self-consecration, — a vital and hallowed *means* of growth. It is now and always *communion* with the Master.

In the mystic language of the Apostle, the Church is the body of Christ, of which he is the living, ever-present Head. Only as each member of that body is inseparably united with him, deriving from him life and support, quickened by his controlling spirit, and impelled by his divine will, can it possess any inherent force, life, or energy. So far only as each member fills his own appointed office, so far as each possesses an individual life, earnest, calm, and controlling, so far as each knows from an inward experience the deep meaning of "a life hid with Christ in God," will the Church of Christ be a *living* Church.

You may form new organizations, you may remodel the outward forms of service, you may erect churches, you may print volumes, you may appoint missionaries and gather new societies, and pour the streams of a profuse benevolence into a thousand channels, — but without this inward life, without this living principle of faith, this love to God and to Christ in the soul, all efforts, all forms, all outward services, will be as the worthless chaff blown away by the passing breeze.

Let, then, every teacher, as he enters on the duties of his office, faithfully examine himself. Let him feel that his example will not have its due weight, nor his teachings their rightful efficacy, and that he is not wholly true to his Master, so long as he neglects those parting words expressive of the desire of affectionate remembrance, so long as he withholds in any measure the weight of his example and influence in promoting the cause of Christ.

Go back in thought to that large upper room, and as one after another the earnest and sorrowing countenances of the disciples pass before you, seek out the one central figure, Him who in sublime self-forgetfulness thinks only of pouring comfort and strength into the troubled hearts of those around him. Place yourself at his feet, and listen to those calm, sublime words of immortal trust and undying affection.

Receive from his lips the parting blessing of his own deep peace and quenchless love; drink in his spirit of divine self-sacrifice; know that your name was borne upon his heart in that hour of love, that his interceding prayer went forth that you also might be made one with him and with the Father; follow him to the garden shades; watch beside him in that hour of dread, mysterious agony; stand with the faithful few beside the cross of suffering and of shame; read there the assurance of pardon and reconciliation; and then turn coldly away, if you can, and slight the last and dying request of your Saviour and your Master!

Some will say, that they do not feel ready to take so decided a stand with regard to the religious life as is usually implied by participation in this service. Remember, though you may *seem* long to halt, there is in reality no middle ground. "No man can serve two masters." The warfare of life must be waged under one of two leaders, — and the choice is your own.

Were Christ visibly present, were he in audible voice to invite those who cherish any degree of love to him, who are *seeking* to be his in heart and life, to partake of his feast of love, would you still turn away from those touching memorials? It *is* his voice that speaks to you, his love that pleads with you, his hand that is stretched forth to welcome you.

Come, then, and be openly, fearlessly, and truly his faithful, loving disciple. Come into the full participation of the blessings vouchsafed to every earnest, humble soul. Come into the close and intimate communion with your Lord and Master.

If you are conscious of the sincere purpose to lead a Christian life, if your prevailing aim and desire be that you may be a faithful disciple of your Saviour, if the love of Christ be in your soul, faint indeed compared with the boundless gratitude which is his due, ye daily deepening and strengthening in the hidden fountains of your being, if you desire to cherish a living faith in him as the Saviour and Redeemer of the soul, then is it indeed said to you, "Come unto me; come gladly, cheerfully, trustingly, — for him that cometh, I will in no wise cast out."

Give to His cause the whole weight of your influence and your example. Be closely united with Him who ever lives as the great Head of the Church. Dwell in intimate union with his spirit, and so walk with him from day to day, that those with whom you are associated shall indeed take knowledge of you, that you have been with Jesus. Then as you go to your duties on the Sabbath, you will speak with new earnestness and power, and the hearts of the young will be through you more deeply impressed with the beauty of holiness and the joy and peace of a reconciled heart.

If you feel that the service would be to you one of mere form; if you feel that you have no

15

peculiar responsibilities to the Church of Christ, no individual relations to him as the Head of that Church; if his love has never glowed within your soul, nor his spirit quickened within you the aspiration for a higher life; if his words have never awakened the cry of a contrite spirit, nor the earnest longings for pardon and reconciliation; if you have never felt your need of a Mediator and Saviour, — then pause, and solemnly answer to yourself the question, "Why am I holding the responsible position of a religious teacher and guide to others? By what right am I, in form at least, seeking to influence the minds of the young, to impart to them the truths of eternal life, unless I know from inward experience something of their power? Am I not thus acting a false part?"

To one side or the other, to God or to the world, do you stand committed. Your own self-judgment must render the true verdict. Postpone not, then, the answer too long. As the solemn scenes of that day rise before you, when the eternal realities of a future being shall stand disclosed to view, when face to face you shall meet Him whose voice has so often pleaded with your inmost soul, resolve so to live, so to unite yourself with his Body, so to confess your Saviour in your daily life and before men, that he will acknowledge you as his before the Father and his angels.

CHAPTER XII.

THE RELATION OF THE CHILD TO THE CHURCH.

"Behold, the covenant is with you and your children."

The relation of the teacher to the Church of Christ is closely and intimately connected with that of the child; but no one conversant with the present state of our schools can fail to be aware of the vague and indefinite feeling that exists among the young respecting this relation, and of the lack of any strong feeling of obligation to observe in a fitting way and season the two simple ordinances of our faith, — Baptism and the Lord's Supper. Apart from other opposing influences, — such as the absence of all home religious instruction, the low standard of character among many who call themselves members of the Body of Christ, the reaction against the use of all outward forms, as if they were necessarily inconsistent with spirituality of faith and practice, — it is not to be denied that much of the present state of coldness and utter indifference is to be ascribed to the defective influence and instruction of our Sunday schools.

Many teachers dismiss the whole subject at once, and consider it as one with which they have no possible connection; while others, faithful in their general teachings, seem to regard it as belonging only to those of mature heart and character, in which the child or youth has no part or interest. He is generally regarded as standing apart, as it were, by himself, outside the pale of the Church, and his ever coming into it is too often left as a wholly optional matter, dependent upon circumstances, taste, or even upon fashion alone.

The result of such training is only too clearly visible. The child grows into the youth, and the youth passes on to maturer years, without being surrounded by any constraining or controlling influence; and as he takes his part in the duties of active life, the Church becomes more and more to him as a mere name, a sort of foreign interest, with which he has not the remotest personal connection, except so far as custom or general opinion demands a half-day attendance on the services of public worship.

Is this state of things right or Christian? Has the *child* no part in the covenant promises of the Redeemer? Is he to be left by himself to wander in the far-off country, until weary and disheartened, filled with remorse and anguish, and heavily laden, he turns back to seek his Father's house? Has not the Church a sacred duty to perform in bringing the young from very infancy into its fold, and so guiding, guarding, and educating them that they shall never wander from its sacred inclosure?

Some may ask, "What is to be understood by the Church, — a word so variously and often so vaguely used?" In the language of another, we reply, "It is that body of persons who believe in Jesus Christ, the Son of God, and Saviour of men, crucified and risen; and so believe in Him as to be personally conscious of a supreme desire to live his spiritual life, to resemble him, and be his true redeemed disciples. Love to God as manifest in Christ, and love to man as God's child, must be the ruling affections in the soul, — whether they have conformed the character perfectly to them or not. The Church is the aggregate of these consecrated souls, aiming and longing above all things, to live righteously; irrespective of names, of forms, of creeds, of age, of place, except so far as these affect this internal, central consecration to Christ. Its boundaries, as it is embodied in actual persons, may be indistinct to man's eye, but they are plain to God's; and the definition is plain. The Church is that body of people, in whatever age or nation, of which Christ is literally and spiritually the Head. And any one particular church is a smaller collection of such people, and so a branch of the Church Universal."

According to the teachings of Christ, and the whole bearing of the New Testament, Baptism formed the initiatory rite, by which new converts to Christianity, or children of Christian believers, were admitted to the privileges and made partakers of the blessings of the Christian faith and covenant. All such were regarded and treated as of the household of faith, and if those baptized in infancy ever denied the covenant-promise implied in this dedicatory rite, made by parents or believing friends, and forsook the guardian care that the Church extended over them, it was through their own willing neglect or wrong-doing.

So should it be now. The child from its first opening years should be led to feel that as he is a member of a particular household, and has his own definite and individual relations to parents, brothers, and sisters, so is he also a member of the Church of Christ, and has his peculiar responsibilities and privileges as such; and that if he ever forfeits them, it must be through his own act.

This view, of course, does not preclude the necessity of the regeneration of individual souls. The child of Christian parents, like all others, needs to have a spiritual life formed within him, in addition to his natural life. Where the child is consecrated from infancy, and educated under Christian influences, such regeneration, the second birth into the new and higher life, *may* very early take place, so that the soul shall grow God-ward and heavenward, even as its bodily powers are developed and strengthened, and he shall never be conscious of the time when he was indifferent to spiritual realities, when the thought of God was not a constraining thought, and the love of Christ a true incentive to action.

If parents and teachers felt more deeply their sacred responsibility thus to train the young spirits committed to their keeping; if the life, the spirit, the teachings of Christ were instilled into the child's soul from very infancy by domestic example, instruction, and family prayer; if he were "often reminded of his Church privileges, and of the joy of his Christian heritage and home," then, as he advanced to maturer years, would he gladly, in every form and way, acknowledge his relation to the Church, and his indebtedness to its one only Head.

As few, very few children are surrounded by such blessed home influences, and brought into the great spiritual Church from earliest childhood; as few, even of those consecrated in infancy by the rite of baptism, are faithfully *edu-*

cated as disciples of Christ, and escape the benumbing influence of the world and of fashion, — the rest must come into membership with the spiritual Church of Christ through the only other mode, that of conversion, of sincere penitence, and of the birth of a Christian conviction, — of a heart dedication to God through Christ.

Whenever the child, the youth, or the person of mature years can distinctly and seriously say, "I am resolved henceforth, through Christ strengthening me, to be a faithful disciple," then does the soul become united with Christ, as a member of his Body or Church.

Both the example and the words of Christ demand that this purpose and this resolve should be confirmed and sealed by outward confession and act. Where the rite of baptism has not been observed in infancy, in which case it is solely the dedicatory act of the parent, bringing the child into covenant relations with the Church, now is the fitting season for the individual to follow his Master's example, and to observe that rite, emblematical of the washing of regeneration, and of the purity of soul to which the disciple aspires, through the putting away of the defilements of sin, and the cleansing and sanctifying influences of the Holy Spirit.

Now is the fitting and true season for him to come to the Lord's table, to express in outward form and by free confession his acknowledgment of his Master's claims upon his gratitude and love, and to consecrate himself unreservedly and openly to his service.

The rite is truly one of remembrance, of *commemoration;* and whenever it can be made such in heart and in spirit, whenever the individual of whatever age is conscious of love to Christ, or of the sincere desire to love him, and wishes thus to commemorate him in the way of his appointment, — then ought he to unite in this service.

To make no distinction between the usual forms of public worship and the observance of this service, to place no difference between the general worship of the congregation and this commemorative rite, would be at once to ignore its peculiar character and purport; for unless it be a service indicative of *individual* affection, love, and gratitude, expressive of the soul's true desire to be brought into a closer harmony with its Redeemer, it becomes at once a mere vain and unmeaning form.

Let no barrier of man's device be placed around the holy table. To very many minds some simple form of personal confession, as the individual first unites in this service, seems right and fitting. "It defines relations, and qualifies for business measures and social action. It is an open, satisfactory step. If it involves a trial of feeling, it is no less acceptable for that cross to Him who bore the cross of an infinitely heavier sacrifice for us. So that, while joining one particular church is also entering into the Church Universal, membership in the Church Universal does not supersede the occasion for special confirmation or confession on the part of those who desire to belong to one portion of that Church in particular."

At the same time, the use of such a form should not be regarded as absolutely essential; for if so regarded, some might absent themselves from the service who would otherwise gladly share in its holy influences; and we are aware that there are those who have conscientious objections to the personal use of any such form. Let each be fully persuaded in his own mind. It is the Lord's table, not man's. It is the Saviour who presides at the feast, and his words of invitation are, " Whosoever *will*, let him freely come."

Let all, then, be freely invited to come who, on their own personal responsibility, feel that they have a part in his covenant-promise; all who regard themselves as Christ's followers, or who are desirous of making him their guide, and are looking to him as their Saviour and Redeemer.

Let the weak come, that they may find strength; the sorrowing, that they may be comforted; the tempted, that they may be sustained; the aged, that they may be blessed; and the young, that they may be gathered into their Redeemer's fold, and have added to the gladsomeness of youth the enduring joy and peace of their Saviour's presence and love, — the assured blessedness of a heart and a life early consecrated to him and his service.

Is it asked what peculiar instructions should be given by the Christian teacher on the observance of these two rites of our faith? We reply, Whether the child be one of believing parents or not, teach him, that, by the very Christian privileges he enjoys in the instructions of the school and the worship of the sanctuary, he holds some definite relations to the Church, and seek, by all possible means, to deepen within his soul the sacred importance of those relations. Converse with him simply and freely. Teach him the true meaning of these rites; explain their import; speak of their privileges. Let every loving and hallowed association cluster around them, and let him not feel as if he were a sort of alien from the true fold, only to be brought within its precincts by some sudden impulse or spasmodic effort in after years; but let the tenderness of a Christian love, and the watchfulness of a Christian heart enfold and guard his earliest years. If in infancy he was consecrated by parental love or Christian friendship to his God and his Saviour, let him be often reminded of his baptismal dedication, and taught to live worthily of it.

Let the school be indeed to him as the school of Christ; and ere he leaves its guardian care, to enter upon the toils and duties and responsibilities of maturer years, let him have been so trained and educated, under the blessing of God and through the sanctifying influences of the Spirit, that in trusting faith and love he shall gladly lay upon the sacred altar of commemoration the offering of his youthful powers and strength, thus dedicating himself upon the threshold of life to his Master's service.

Thus, and thus only, will the school become a true co-worker with the Church in the Christian education of the young, and in the regeneration of individual souls. Thus only shall we educate those now pupils to become teachers worthy of their vocation; for only so far as teachers are themselves living members of the Church of Christ, only so far as they are laboring to bring the young into the one great fold of the Redeemer, only so far is any school worthy to bear the name of its one Master and Head,— worthy of being called a Christian institution.

" The Spirit, in our hearts,
Is whispering, ' Sinner, come ! '
The Bride, the Church of Christ, proclaims
To all his children, ' Come ! '

" Let him that heareth say
To all about him, Come !

Let him that thirsts for righteousness
  To Christ, the fountain, come!

"Yes, *whosoever will*,
  O let him freely come,
And freely drink the stream of life:
  'T is Jesus bids him come."

CHAPTER XIII.

THE CHRISTIAN STANDARD OF CHARACTER.

"Nearer, my God, to thee,
Nearer to thee!
E'en though it be a cross
That raiseth me;
Still all my song would be,
Nearer, my God, to thee,
Nearer to thee!"

THE questions are sometimes asked "whether the Sunday school is to be regarded as a *permanent* institution, and how far it is to be considered as an effective and true co-worker with the Church." The answer to each of these questions is one and the same.

The permanence and the usefulness of such schools will ever be in exact proportion to the degree in which they are made peculiarly and emphatically *religious* schools. Just so far as they are imbued with spiritual life and an inward energy; just so far as the spirit of Christ is diffused throughout the whole system, and his reconciling offices as Mediator and Saviour are felt to be a reality; just so far as the words of Gospel truth are received into the soul as fountains of life, — just so far, and no farther, will they be self-sustained and secure, — the means of a high spiritual growth.

Let our schools be characterized by no high aims, no vital sense of their dependence on, and intimate union with, the great Head of the Church; let them be mere intellectual institutions, the teachers imparting a knowledge of Gospel truth much in the same way as they would a lesson from Euclid; let them to any degree do away with home religious instruction, or lessen the sense of parental responsibility, as is sometimes the case, — and the sooner they are closed the better.

That changes and réforms are needed among us, that we have a right to expect higher influences and a more spiritual life to go forth from our schools, that we are to look to those educated beneath their influence to be the most faithful supporters of the Church and the most active in all plans of benevolent enterprise, few will deny.

Any change, any improvement, any real and permanent good to be effected, must begin at the fountain-head. The true life of our Schools, as they exist to-day, *depends wholly on the religious life of the teachers of to-day.*

Let teachers be, in spirit and in life, consecrated to their Master's service, willing to forego ease and self-indulgence to promote his work, — earnest in self-improvement, counting it all joy if in God's way, and not merely according to their own choice, they may labor in his vineyard and win souls to Christ, feeling the Saviour's presence as a constant incentive to duty, and waiting on the Spirit as the sustainer and sanctifier of the soul, — then shall a power and an influence go forth from among us to rouse the indifferent and careless, to break down the strongholds of sin and iniquity, to purify the streams of fashion and worldliness, to bring the ignorant and wandering into the fold of Christ, to shed light over the dark places of human misery and guilt, and to render many a barren and desolate waste as the garden of the Lord.

Then would children be nurtured in the beauty of holiness, and early brought into covenant relations with their Redeemer. Then would the Church arise and shine, and put on her beautiful garments, and the ways of Zion would no longer mourn because so few come to her solemn feasts; for the Saviour's animating presence would no longer be held by any heart as a dim and beautiful tradition of the past, but his constraining love and the quickening impulse of his divine spirit would be welcomed and cherished as the soul's richest heritage.

There is one danger to which even the truly Christian teacher is exposed, one evil through which the sincerely consecrated heart is liable to lose sight of its lofty aims and its immortal inheritance, — an evil showing itself in so many thousand different ways, and revealing its potent influence under such diverse forms, that to enumerate them would be impossible, and yet which mars many an otherwise Christ-like character and noble spirit; — we refer to the danger and the evil of the abounding, potent, everywhere prevalent spirit of worldliness; a spirit which not only asserts its sway in the market, the exchange, the counting-room, the gay and fashionable party, but which presses itself into the sanctuary of home, intrudes upon the secret hours of devotion, paralyzes the noblest forms of benevolence, and tends to reverse the divine standard of the Gospel, which for ever proclaims the supremacy of the inward over the outward, and the unseen over the seen and perishable. Its constant and universal tendency is, *to lower the standard of personal attainment*, to degrade holiness into mere outward morality, the faith of the heart into a mere intellectual belief, and righteousness into a decent conformity with the usages of the world. The divine image of purity and truth becomes marred, and by degrees the holiness of Christ is regarded, not only as beyond the attainment, but even as beyond the earnest aspiration, of the spirit. The Saviour's earnest and emphatic words, "Ye cannot serve God and Mammon," come to be regarded as a paradox, and the sharp conflict between the world and God, between pride and self-sufficiency and the eternal power and unchangeable holiness of the Divine will, is earnestly waged, as if outward decency could take the place of inward piety, and the plans and activity and might of man could work out for him an eternal salvation; as if, to the Divine eye, there were no clearly marked distinction between a correct, upright deportment, induced more by circumstances than by choice, and a heart consecrated to God and to Christ.

What is the only standard which the Gospel recognizes, and which Christ requires? "Be ye perfect, even as your Father is perfect." "Be ye holy, for I am holy."

"Abide in me," said the Saviour, "and I in you, for without me ye can do nothing." And how deep the mystic and hidden meaning of the Apostle's words, "For ye are dead, and your life is hid with Christ in God!" Far more do they imply than a mere mechanical conformity to the usages of society, and the standard of the world, or a ready compliance with the force of circumstances and of education. They speak of a power at work in the very depths of the soul, a power to transform, and to renew; of motives to effort, to duty, and to obedience, of which the world takes no cognizance, but which, when inwrought into the soul, clothe it as with a giant's strength, and invest it with a superhuman power. They imply a heart at one with Christ, permeated by his divine life, his spirit prompting every true feeling and noble exertion; a will in entire harmony with his, never seeking its own purposes, but moved, swayed, and governed by the divine. They speak of a soul freed from self, living only in and through Christ, and consecrated to him, not only for life, but for eternity; — a soul so consecrated that it shall be willing to be buffeted even in its highest desires, if thus it shall be made more lowly, and brought nearer the divine humility of the Saviour. It is equally ready to suffer as to act; to serve in silence, pain, or loneliness, as on the busy theatre of life; for the life is but the spontaneous expression of its purest love, which asks nothing from others, claims nothing for itself, but rejoices that in any way it can labor for Christ, or express its gratitude and affection.

Is such an attainment easy? Is it to be won by cold endeavors, faint aspirations, occasional longings, and heartless prayers? Has it nothing to combat in the low standard of worldly goodness, and self-righteous morality? — no fearful word of rebuke for self-satisfied indolence, no trumpet tongue to arouse the slumbering soul from its death-like trance of self-complacent worldliness? Has it no emphatic voice of warning, no quickening word of power, to him who would guide others in the way of life, who seeks to point the young, the ardent, the aspiring soul to the nobler heights of Christian attainment and heavenly goodness?

There is nothing, as some might imagine, strange, forced, or unnatural in a life like this. It is simply and only following Christ in daily duty, walking with him, looking constantly to him for guidance and help, acknowledging his claims as the Master of the soul, and yielding to him the ready and glad obedience he requires. A child can understand the meaning, and recognize the beauty of this life of holiness; while the faithful Christian of threescore years and ten, whose brow may seem to others visibly encircled as with a crown of glory, will feel that he has but taken his first steps heavenward, so constantly will the Divine image manifested in Christ grow upon his soul, ever revealing nobler and nobler heights of attainment.

"Blessed are they who do *hunger* and *thirst* after righteousness"; for the promise is alone to those who would gladly feed on that living Bread which came down from heaven, and who truly thirst for the pure waters of life, that "they shall be filled."

> "O, sacred union with the Perfect Mind!
>   Transcendent bliss, which thou alone canst give!
> How blest are they this pearl of price who find,
>   And, dead to earth, have learned in thee to live!
>
> "O go, and learn this lesson of the cross,
>   And tread the way which saints and prophets trod,

Who, counting life and self and all things loss,
Have found in inward death the life of God."

Go forth, then, Christian teacher, to your duties, fully and freely recognizing your *high calling;* for only through this deep religious life, only through souls thus consecrated, will our schools become worthy the support of Christian hearts, worthy the fostering and guardian care of the Church, or worthy to bear the name of their divine Master.

Go forth with vigor, with earnestness, and with a living faith in the eternal word of promise. Go forth, nerved as with a divine impulse, to labor in the vineyard, restrained by no false doubts or unworthy misgivings. Go, charged with something of the noble Christian energy that animated Gordan Hall, when he offered to work his way to the field; with the earnest zeal and trusting faith through which the faithful Crocker adopted, as his only motto of life, "What ought to be done can be done, Christ strengthening us"; with the unquenchable ardor and consecrated energy of the devoted Brainerd, who so early rested from his labors in the earthly vineyard of his Lord.

Above all, go forth in the spirit and the name of Christ. Though discouragements are around you, though trials encompass your path, though you may witness no present results of your labors, hesitate not to tread even the rough path

of duty, for Christ dwells ever at your side. Like the beloved disciple, lean on his breast; cling to his supporting hand, kneel humbly at his feet. Enter into a true and living fellowship with him, that you may know, from glad experience, the meaning of "a life hid with Christ in God."

Obey the Saviour's parting command, first and chief of all, by preaching the truth through a Christ-like life and conversation, by being yourself a living gospel, known and read of all men.

Proclaim the words of truth, not alone on the Sabbath hour, and to the few gathered in your class, but regard it as your noblest privilege, in any way or form, to make known the power and the blessedness of the Gospel of Christ. According as you have found him precious to your own soul, so speak in confidence and faith to the young, the erring, or the tempted. Dwell in daily communion with your God and your Saviour, and through the deep life of lowly prayer so realize the great truths of your inward being that other souls shall feel the quickening influences of your spirit, and your words shall be vital with a divine power and energy. Look upward, and catch the inspiring glance of the Master's eye, and hear the thrilling sound of his voice, as in tender love he bids even the little children come to him, — and then, in the child's spirit and the child's faith, receive the proffered blessing.

Remember, that, should your convictions of truth and of duty ever lead you to a solitary path of effort, you are not laboring alone, for if but faithful to your own soul, all the great forces of the spiritual universe are pledged in your behalf. Remember the great cloud of witnesses by which you are surrounded, not only the earnest and true of past times, but those whose faithful lives and loving spirits have blessed our own homes and schools, and left in many hearts the sacred memories of their Christ-like walk and conversation.

Not alone have they left us to labor; for though hid from mortal sight, their spirits still abide with us in the fellowship of faith and of love, bidding us to strive as they have striven, to trust as they have trusted, and still to faint not in well-doing

Go forth, then, Christian teacher, casting aside once and for ever all coldness, all indifference, all low aims and merely worldly standards of excellence. Consecrate yourself in heart and life, in soul and strength, to your Redeemer's service. Enter into covenant relations with your soul's only Saviour. Seek the constant help and the sanctifying influences of the Spirit. Lean upon the Father's proffered support and blessing. And when called into the more immediate presence of the Great Shepherd of souls, may you experience a glad reunion with the little flock here committed to your keeping; may you be enabled, with humble confidence and a trusting faith, to render up the account of your sacred stewardship; and being found faithful unto death, may you receive from the Master's hands the crown of life.

May your witness be in heaven, and your record on high!

THE END.

www.ingramcontent.com/pod-product-compliance
Lightning Source LLC
LaVergne TN
LVHW011221110826
845150LV00006B/1498

9781425515454